RIGHTLY DIVIDING THE WORD OF TRUTH

II TIMOTHY 2:15 "STUDY TO SHEW THYSELF APPROVED UNTO GOD, A WORKMAN THAT NEEDED NOT TO BE ASHAMED, RIGHTLY DIVIDING THE WORD OF TRUTH."

TODAY'S PASTORS,

To Stay or Run©

Written by: Christopher E. Howe

This book is dedicated to all Pastors, Evangelists, Missionaries, Preachers, and all those who feel the call to preach on their lives. May you find some fundamental truths from the bible in this book as we seek the Lord for his guidance in ministry. You are loved

Special thanks to Barbara Lippincott-Lonsky for her tireless efforts in editing this book.

All scripture references are from the King James Version of the bible. The scripture references are bold, italicized, or underlined for emphasis

Index

Introduction

Ministry is a difficult calling at times. It is one that can be heart- breaking, frustrating, and depressing, as the Pastor must carry the burdens of the church as a whole, plus, the burdens of his own family. The call to be a Pastor must be one that has come from God himself, as he is the one that calls. God will also provide a way for you to be able to handle the task to which you are assigned.

The Pastors of today are so much different than the pastors of yesterday in that, the pastors of today are not taught to hold the course to endure to the end. I hear all the time in the pastorate of Pastors wanting to retire, or those looking forward to retirement, If not retirement, they want to go on to bigger, and better churches.

There are many pastors out there today that have multiple churches on their resumes. The pastors have all this "experience" in the ministry yet, when the going gets tough, my dear reader friend, the going will get tough, these pastors run, and quit.

I look at things a little more old school, I have only been in the pastorate about five years, I have seen and heard of many quitting the task, and nowhere in the bible does it say or even give an example of a pastor, minister, prophet, priest, apostle, disciple, ever retiring or quitting. They performed their tasks until their last breath, or until their physical bodies could not possibly handle it any longer.

In the bible believing churches of today, this perseverance is something that is lacking. The pastor comes to a church expecting that he can build the church. The pressures are put on him by the church, and often the pastor is terrified of the church, or in modern churches, the board firing them. Our church is a Pastor led church as the bible establishes it to be, not a board led church as many are today. My dear reader friend, if you are a God-called pastor, and you worry about a board of elders firing you, then you are not trusting God like you need to. If God put you there he will protect you there.

I am, what you might call, an old school pastor. I believe, in faith, that if I do the tasks that God has placed on me, and do those things that God will do what he says he will do. (If I do, He Will). I have learned over the few years that I have been a pastor, that it is not my responsibility to build the church. It is not my responsibility to save souls, or change lives, that, my dear reader friend, is God's job. My job is to plant, sow, water, and nurture the seed of the gospel. My job is not to put butts in the seat. I still believe in the power of the bible. I believe Hebrews 4:12 that tells us that the bible is (quick) or alive and powerful. I believe Isaiah 55:11 where the bible says that the word of the Lord will not return void. God's word will not return without fruit. The problem with the pastors of today is that they have become hirelings, and not God-called pastors.

I am on many different sites on social media listing churches that need pastors, just to keep informed about things going on. All of the searching churches want Pastors to have qualifications in certain things. Churches want pastors that have degrees from man-made colleges, credentials from those degrees are confirmed based on some misinterpreted passages designed for bishops, and not for the requirements of a pastor, that God has set forth in the book of Jeremiah. Nowhere in this list of requirements, do I ever see a church that is looking for a God-called pastor. It seems being God-called is no longer a requirement for the pastorate in today's world. That, dear friend, is the first step in the failure of churches seeking pastors.

On the flip side of the coin, I see Pastors looking for churches that will support them at sixty to seventy thousand dollars a year, provide them medical benefits, and retirement plans. These candidates want all these things and they treat the pastorate like a corporate job. When did the apostle Paul treat his calling like a business? When did the prophet Elijah ask God for a retirement plan? Those men of God did not. They went as God said for them to go, they had nothing. The Lord met every need along the way.

The biggest problem I see about pastors seeking churches, which really frustrates me, is that they post online, and tell everyone that "God has called them to be a pastor." Stating "They are willing to go to any church that God leads them to. " These pastors say they will do anything that God asks them to do, as long as it is in the area where they live so they can still stay close to family, to their jobs, and to keep their houses."

In this day and age, a Pastor feels they must buy a house before they can do what God has called them to do. Pastors of today are no longer living by or operating their ministry by faith, but by sight. This my dear friend, is why the ministry is suffering, and the pastors, the shepherds, are leaving by the handful. The pastors quit because they do not have a foundation built on faith in the Lord, but on their sight in what they can or cannot do.

This book will discuss many different topics of the pastorate, it is not intended to slam the pastor, as I am one! The intent is to encourage the pastor that is truly a God-called pastor to live by faith. We must take the punches of the ministry, and let God do what he can do so we can receive the victory through the Lord Jesus Christ.

It is my intent that his book will be an interesting read as it will show what the bible says on all issues discussed. It is then, my dear reader friend that you, and you alone, will have to make your choice to either believe the bible for what it says, and receive the victory, or you will have to choose to reject the bible for what it says, and live by sight. Living by sight you will never succeed for the Lord.

If I can ever be of any assistance to you at all please feel free to contact me. My contact info will be on the last page of this book, PASTOR, my dear friend, please do not quit, please keep on keeping on, you are not alone.

You are loved.

Pastor Chris Howe

TO LIVE BY FAITH

Hebrews 11:6
But without faith it is impossible to please him: for he that cometh to God must believe that he is, and that he is a rewarder of them that diligently seek him.

I believe that one of the most difficult concepts for the pastors of today, and even the pastors of yesterday, is living by faith. We have all lived in a society that has conditioned us to live by sight. It is the "Lone Ranger" so to speak, that truly steps out in faith to serve the Lord. In the bible all they had was faith, and we saw how God moved in mighty ways. Ever wonder why we no longer see the foundations in our churches shake? Ever wonder what happened to the power that Elijah had on Mount Carmel? All those mighty acts were done by faith, a power that we no longer utilize.

We do things in our own strength today, and from time to time we credit God for doing big things when in reality, we have faith in ourselves. For example, we pray for the Lord to give us a larger building. We pray, and pray, and we wait for a little bit. Then we go to the bank, and get a loan to build that big building. We say "Hallelujah! God provided that building!" No my dear pastor friend, YOU provided that building.

If God provided that building you would be debt free, and not have that excessive mortgage consuming your building, and general funds. Now, you may have to compromise the fundamentals of the bible to keep the people in the church that give money to pay for the building. I believe it is great practice for a church to remain debt free, after all isn't it God's church? Didn't Jesus say that upon this rock he will build his church? Then my dear pastor friend let him build it.

I am not against new buildings, nice stuff in the building, and even multiple locations if that was what the Lord wanted, but nowhere in the bible do we see any man of God running to the bank, or to other people for loans. Nowhere in the bible do we see Pastors compromising on things to make others happy. One thing for sure, when the church is debt free, and owes nothing, and the church, and the pastor are living, and doing ministry by faith, you can preach, and teach the bible for what it says. A pastor can preach it hard, you can preach about hell, the lake of fire, repentance, and how bad a person is, and that they need Jesus, without worrying about paying the mortgage.

When a church has loans they preach on the love of God, making the people feel good. The pastor tells them they are good as long as they have a relationship of some kind with Jesus. They bring forth the service with fancy lights, and small little choruses to generate a religious experience. The indebted church never preaches the stuff that's going to convict men's hearts to get right with God. Why is this?

When Jesus came unto his own, his own received him not. The people were offended by his truth.

The bible tells us that there is nothing new under the sun, and my dear pastor friend, nothing has changed. Over half of the people that faithfully attend churches in the United States alone, would up and leave, the moment Pastors preached the truth of the bible.

It is crucial for a pastor to be willing to live by faith, it is faith that honors God, it is faith that moves the mountains in our lives, it is faith that hits the very heart of God. Any truly God-called pastor out there will have to battle his fleshly desires. The pastor will step himself and his family out on blind faith, and blind faith alone, to do what God has for them to do. That is the way to tell a truly God-called pastor from a hireling.

There are many pastors out there today that are just filling a space in the church. They want benefits, money, houses, and cars, etc. What these pastors fail to realize is that the office of a pastor in the church is one that the Lord takes very seriously. God says he will give pastors after his own heart to feed his sheep.

The office of pastor in the church is accountable to God, not a board of elders, but to God alone. When a person is in the pastoral role and they are not living and operating by faith, they, my friend, are held doubly accountable to God. First for not living by faith, and second for being in a God called position, and not doing it God's way.

My leaps of faith have been big, they have been scary, they have left us almost stranded at times, however, God always provided. God made a way, and each and every time I learn to trust him a little more. I learned that you don't need large bank accounts, that you don't need a million-dollar building, with many thousands a year in payroll. I have learned that if you live by faith, operate the church on faith that if you let God run his church his way, it is the best way. Faith also teaches you that it is not your job to build God's church, that is God's job.

I challenge you to go on some of the "pastors looking for churches" sites on the internet. You will find thousands of pastors looking to pastor churches. At the same time you will find thousands of churches needing pastors. I ask myself, why is this the case?

As I read these sites, I look at the expectations of the pastors. Most of them will say they are called by God to pastor churches. These pastors say they will do whatever God wants for them to do. The pastors are looking for the church that God wants for them but when you talk to them, they are not willing to leave their homes, and the area that they live in. They are not willing to leave that corporate job to take a small, or non-salaried job to run that little country church. These pastors are not willing to sell all they have, and take up their cross and follow Jesus. They are not truly God called but man-called, man-pleasing. These men have a form of godliness, wanting to serve God, but not the power to back it up. It is the pastor that is truly seeking God that will step out on faith, and get things done for the Lord.

I can say this with the authority of God's word and by my own experience. I moved my family on faith twice across the country to do the ministry that God had for me to do. The first time was from Florida to Colorado to start a church, which ended up being a homeless ministry. This work was my bootcamp ministry. I had faith in the Lord, but not as much trust as I should have had. I had to learn to trust the Lord while serving in Colorado.

When the Lord called us to pastor where we are now, we blindly, on faith, moved from Colorado to New York to pastor a church of only six people with no salary. Man, what a blessing it has been to watch God provide each and every thing. Yes, I have to work and pastor a church at the same time, but my bible says that Paul, and Peter did the same thing. Where is that faith today, my dear pastor friend? Where are those men that step out on faith for the Lord, calling unto him to do great and mighty things which we know not? (Jeremiah 33:3) Where is your faith in the Lord, my dear pastor friend?

As always, in all my books, let's not take what I am saying, and run with it. I am just a sinner saved by God's amazing grace, serving him in the role to which he has called me. I will say, I believe with every ounce of my being, that old tried, and true, proven over, and over again, and still found faithful King James Bible. That is where my faith comes from. So let's see what the bible has to say. You can either accept the bible for what it says or you can deny it, that is your choice, either way I will still be your friend.

Romans 10:17
So then faith cometh by hearing, and hearing by the word of God. As we have been saying, it is the bible, the word of God that leads a person to Christ. It is the bible, the word of God that increases one's faith in God. It is being in the bible every day that makes our faith grow stronger.

When I first started out as a pastor I used to read commentaries, and get my understanding from them. Yes, I believed the bible for what it said but, I was not disciplined enough to read just the bible. One day, the Holy Spirit convicted my heart about looking at commentaries, and I chose to use the bible only and an old time English dictionary. Man, when I did that, it was so much better. I found my style of preaching changing, from okay to hard core, I found the presence of the Holy Spirit in the messages stronger than ever before, I found my hatred for sin growing stronger, and my love for others increasing.

I realized that the closer I got to the bible the more the fruits of the Spirit began to define who I am in Christ Jesus. I have such a long way to go still, but the more I am in the bible the more I begin to spot the fallacies of bible-denying religions, the falseness of man-made doctrine, and the truth of the bible. My convictions for the things of God began to increase, and I began to be resolved to follow the things of God. It is all through the bible, because all of the bible is inspired by God. The bible is quick (alive) and powerful, and its truth is only revealed through the Holy Spirit to the saved person who is truly seeking the Lord.

Hebrews 11:6
But without faith it is impossible to please him: for he that cometh to God must believe that he is, and that he is a rewarder of them that diligently seek him. Whether intentional or not, when a pastor begins to do ministry without basing it on faith, they end up just doing it for themselves. Their labour becomes in vain. The only way to please God is to operate on faith.

Living by faith is such a hard thing for many people to do. As we saw in the last verse, the only way to increase, and strengthen that faith is through the bible. Many pastors quit the ministry because they have lost the vision of the gospel. They have been side tracked by the disappointments, and the hurts of people, and especially from the people they felt were their biggest supporters. The difference between a God-called pastor and man-pleasing pastor (an hireling) is the God-called pastor will hold the course while the man-pleasing pastor will quit and run when the going gets tough, or the next bigger church comes along.

Faith will allow the pastor to navigate through the trials, and the hurts of this world, and will help them to hold the course. Look at Peter and Paul in the book of Acts. How many times were they beaten, thrown into prison? Their ministry was not of their own efforts, if it were they would have quit because they would have only been serving their own purposes. When faith is involved, and is sought for, that my dear pastor friend, is what keeps us going.

The many pastors today who quit or "retire" in my opinion, have had their faith shaken at some point, and have some frustrations, and hurt built up that caused them to do ministry out of obligation, and not out of faith in the Lord or in their calling to pastor. Being in the bible, increasing, and strengthening your faith, will not allow you to be shaken in the faith. By faith, you will endure the hurts, you will suffer greatly at times, but that faith in the Lord will keep you going so you can please God, because without faith it is IMPOSSIBLE to please God. I will address my comment on "retire" in a later chapter.

2 Corinthians 5:7
(For we walk by faith, not by sight:) This verse lays out the biblical plan for our service to the Lord we are to live by faith not by sight. When a pastor seeks only to pastor a church that will pay him certain salaries, pay for his medical, pay for his retirement plan, and whatever other things they want, they are NOT living by faith.

If a church offers to pay a pastor, that is great, but to say I'm not going to pastor that church because they cannot pay me this or that, then that my friend, is not walking by faith, it is walking by selfish desires. I have debated this issue of pastors seeking compensation for ministry in my heart, for a while. When comparing the pastor's expectation of compensation to the men of the bible, we see the bible examples set before us. Paul, and others did not ask for compensation, but obeyed God's command to go and tell others by faith, to have faith in God.

The apostles did not beckon God for salaries, houses, retirement plans or even medical benefits, because the Lord told them that he would meet their needs along the way. God would provide for them as they went. These God called men had enough faith in the Lord that they feared not being in the center of God's will by not fulfilling the call that God put on their lives.

Step back my dear pastor friend, and see how the churches, and the pastors today have so commercialized the calling of God that they want to negotiate the call of God before they fulfill it. They want to treat it like a job and not a calling. I have not yet come across one church that is looking for a God-called pastor. Nor have I found one Pastor yet, that is looking for a church who is willing to go anywhere that

God may call them without any compensation by faith alone, if that is where God wants them. What happened to our faith today? We are to LIVE by FAITH, NOT by sight.

Acts 6:1-8
And in those days, when the number of the disciples was multiplied, there arose a murmuring of the Grecians against the Hebrews, because their widows were neglected in the daily ministration. 2. Then the twelve called the multitude of the disciples unto them, and said, It is not reason that we should leave the word of God, and serve tables. The twelve apostles were being burdened with the complaints of the ministry about some people being neglected in the work of the Lord. The apostles are telling this crowd that they have their job to do. Pastor we cannot do everything. We have certain responsibilities, and we need to delegate some things to others to get the work of the Lord going, which he has called us to do.

3. Wherefore, brethren, look ye out among you seven men of honest report, full of the Holy Ghost and wisdom, whom we may appoint over this business. 4. But we will give ourselves continually to prayer, and to the ministry of the word. The apostles' job is a lot like our job as pastors. The pastor's job is to give ourselves continually to prayer and the work of the ministry. It is faith that keeps us going in the ministry God has called us to.

5. And the saying pleased the whole multitude: and they chose Stephen, a man full of faith and of the Holy Ghost, and Philip, and Prochorus, and Nicanor, and Timon, and Parmenas, and Nicolas a proselyte of Antioch: 6. Whom they set before the

apostles: and when they had prayed, they laid their hands on them. 7. And the word of God increased; and the number of the disciples multiplied in Jerusalem greatly; and a great company of the priests were obedient to the faith. 8. And Stephen, full of faith and power, did great wonders and miracles among the people. Notice here it says that the priests were obedient to the faith and that Stephen was FULL of faith, and as a result of him being full of that faith the Lord used him to accomplish great wonders, and miracles. It is through faith we can accomplish great things, but faith is the one thing that has been removed from the ministry today. The pastor of today has no idea what living, and operating by faith is actually about. The modern pastor has no idea how to suffer for the cause of Christ, he has no idea how to pastor God's church,

I see people online selling books on how to build your church in one year, and how to go from twenty to two hundred in the church in a matter of weeks. These folks probably can do this for some period of time, but they will all compromise the faith, deny the truth of the bible, and diminish the power of Jesus. You may say. "Pastor Chris, that is not a fair statement. " I will say. "Ok then. How is it that a man can build a church of thousands in a manner of weeks, preaching only the bible and the truth of the bible without compromise?"

The bible tells us that the world will hate us because they hated Jesus first, Jesus came unto his own and his own rejected him. People will not listen to the truth in the last days, the bible tells us this. The bible also tells us that God is the same yesterday, today, and forever, the bible goes on to tell us that there is nothing new under the sun. So with all that being said, if a man builds a church from twenty to two thousand in a manner of weeks, then he has had to compromise the things of God somewhere. This does NOT include those truly bible believing churches that have allowed God to build his church over time, over years.

1 Corinthians 16:13

Watch ye, stand fast in the faith, quit you like men, be strong. One of the definitions of Quit simply defined is: *to behave a certain way*. The bible is saying in this verse that we are to hold to the faith, we are to cling to the faith, we are to act like men, be brave like men, stand, and endure hardships like men. Notice it says to hold fast the faith before it says to act like men, and be strong, because it is only faith that makes one strong in the Lord. The faith that makes one hold on is only through faith in the bible, and being in the bible every day. The churches of America, and the pastors of America today have not had to suffer for the things of God. They quit, and run, they leave, and do not cleave to the things of God. My dear pastor friend, if I can encourage you in any way, please, please, cleave to the faith in the Lord, let the Lord Jesus Christ guide you through this, and see the victory your heart desires through Jesus Christ.

Galatians 2:20

I am crucified with Christ: nevertheless I live; yet not I, but Christ liveth in me: and the life which I now live in the flesh I live by the faith of the Son of God, who loved me, and gave himself for me. Paul tells us that he is crucified, he is suffering the trials of this world, that people are hating him, they are beating him, they are trying to kill him, but he is living by the faith, not by the sight, of the Son of God. It is through faith that Paul is able to endure these hardships, that he is able to suffer for the things of

God. It is during these times of trials, and suffering that a God called man begins to realize the depth of God's love.

If we, as people, never had to suffer hardships, we would forget all about where God saved us from, and it would make things all about us. Today's pastor runs from the hardships. These men do not endure until the end, they lack the understanding of who God is, and they forget what God saved them from. Remember, Paul asked God to remove this affliction from him, three times, and God said no, because his grace was sufficient for him? It is because affliction reminds us of who God is. Affliction allows us to cling to that old rugged cross, it is affliction that helps us do what needs to be done for the Lord with the Lord getting the glory for it all, while at the same time, God blesses you in ways you had never imagined.

Colossians 2:7-8
Rooted and built up in him, and stablished in the faith, as ye have been taught, abounding therein with thanksgiving. 8. Beware lest any man spoil you through philosophy and vain deceit, after the tradition of men, after the rudiments of the world, and not after Christ. Rooted in him, rooted in Jesus Christ. Notice it says stablished in the faith which means established. We are to be rooted in Jesus Christ, grounded in the faith.

Being established in the faith means that our faith will hold throughout the course of time. Being stablished in the faith will allow us to endure until the end. To do so we must be in the bible every day, meditating on the things of God, pondering what the bible has to say, and seeking the Lord diligently every day to keep being stablished in the faith. It is faith and only faith that establishes one for the Lord. It is our responsibility as pastors to be in the word, to be in the bible, to be seeking intentionally the things of God. We are to set the example for others to follow. This is the job that God has assigned to us, yes, many will come saying they are called, but time will tell.

Hebrews 10:21-25
And having an high priest over the house of God; 22. Let us draw near with a true heart in full assurance of faith, having our hearts sprinkled from an evil conscience, and our bodies washed with pure water. 23. Let us hold fast the profession of our faith without wavering; (for he is faithful that promised;) This is something that those that do not seek the Lord through faith miss. God is FAITHFUL that promised. God is always able to provide exceedingly, and abundantly above all that our minds could ever imagine. He is able to do, and he will, as he has promised, do!

This passage here tells us to draw near to God in faith, seek him, long for him. My dear pastor friend, is your faith shaken, have you had those thoughts of quitting, are you longing for retirement here on this earth? I want to challenge you to take some time off, and seek God like never before. Seek him, long for him, and let God do what he is going to do. He will restore your hope, he will give you that renewed love for him.

Then verse twenty-three goes on to say that we need to hold fast our profession of our faith, this simply defined is we need to cling to the things of God, we need to cling to our faith, we need to be seeking God like never before, and let the Lord do what only he can do. I heard a statement once that says "a tested faith, is a trusted faith" if your faith has never been tested, it cannot be trusted.

James 1:1-8
James, a servant of God and of the Lord Jesus Christ, to the twelve tribes which are scattered abroad, greeting. 2. My brethren, count it all joy when ye fall into divers temptations; 3. Knowing this, that the trying of your faith worketh patience. 4. But let patience have her perfect work, that ye may be perfect and entire, wanting nothing. This passage is telling us that we are to count it all joy when the trials of this world come up. We are to count it all joy when we suffer for the things of God. It is during these times that we begin to see the glory of God on a totally different level.

As I am writing this section, the Holy Spirit has reminded me, that a couple of years ago I told the Lord that I no longer wanted his okay-ness in my life. I wanted his best. I wanted that kind of faith, and power that Elijah, Moses, Abraham and other men in the bible had. I want that fire coming down from heaven kind of praying, that mountain moving kind of faith. As I have been on that journey, I have learned that this kind of faith only comes from enduring trials, suffering, and it builds endurance. The trying of our faith works patience. These trials make us long for the things of God, and that builds our patience. This patience is our resolve to stay the course, not waver from the faith, to hold on, and find that rest in the Lord

Notice it also says that once that patience has had her perfect work, that we will be wanting nothing as God will provide all that is needed. We will find everything we need in the Lord. As I am often asked by my wife, what do you want for Christmas or for your birthday? I honestly tell her nothing. I have all I want in Christ Jesus and in her. That is it. We need to get to the point that the Lord is all we need to do what the Lord has asked us to do. He will bless, and supply in ways you can never imagine here in this life.

5. If any of you lack wisdom, let him ask of God, that giveth to all men liberally, and upbraideth not; and it shall be given him. 6. But let him ask in faith, nothing wavering. For he that wavereth is like a wave of the sea driven with the wind and tossed. 7. For let not that man think that he shall receive any thing of the Lord. 8. A double minded man is unstable in all his ways. The bible is clear that we are to seek the wisdom of God. This wisdom comes from the bible. When we ask God to grant us wisdom, he will. Wisdom, godly wisdom, is only from God. We must ask him to give us this wisdom through faith, and faith alone. It is faith that moves the things of God, and makes them manifest. It is faith that draws the person seeking God closer to God.

The bible tells us to ask for faith not wavering. It is not saying, I have faith in the Lord here, but not there. What about that pastor that has faith to go where God has called him, but then lives by sight trying to build his church thinking he is doing it God's way. Those that are not in their bibles as they should be will not have that unwavering faith, they will be double minded. Those that waver will not have faith at times, for the simple things they might have faith. The bible tells us that if any man is to receive anything from the Lord he is to receive it on faith, he is to receive it through the power and provision of God. If his faith is wavering, his ministry will waver.

My dear pastor friend, please hold the course of your faith, do not waver. Do not waste many hours in prayer longing for something from God and not receive it because your faith was shaken. Those things you ask for are not given because you did not believe in faith that God was going to do what he said he would do. Please do not waver, do not quit, do not leave. Please cleave to the things of God, and the calling that God has placed on your life to be a pastor.

UNDERSTANDING YOUR CALL

John 15:16
Ye have not chosen me, but I have chosen you, and ordained you, that ye should go and bring forth fruit, and that your fruit should remain: that whatsoever ye shall ask of the Father in my name, he may give it you.

The position of a pastor in a church must be a God-called position or one will never succeed in the ministry. Many pastors will have physical success, they may have thousands of people coming to church, they may have five pastors in their church and have a multi-million-dollar budget, with two or three campuses, the question is, does that make them successful spiritually?

What about that small country church that has about twenty-five or so people attending? The church is debt free, the pastor is not receiving a salary, and has to work a job. Would some consider them successful? These are questions that we must explore for a bit to find out what the difference is between a God-called pastor and a man-pleasing pastor.

A God-called pastor is one that the Lord has pressed upon the heart. Most of the time that person does not want to go, and be a pastor but, is a person that is trying with all his soul to seek God, and the things of the Lord. Many good pastors have been God called. This call from God to be a Pastor is something that is not seen so much today. Because of the commercialization of the pastorate, that the call of God gets overlooked. Pastors don't care about the call of God on them, and most churches are looking for pastors today that do not have the qualification of being "God-called" as a requirement for being a pastor.

This God-called person will be the one that is seeking God in prayer. He will be the one that is in the bible and making it part of his life. This God-called pastor will be the one that if God impresses on his heart to move across the country with no job or place to live to pastor a church with no money, and six people, he moves across the country, and pastors a church with six people, and does as the Holy Spirit has impressed him to do.

This man will be the one that holds strong to the faith of the bible, he will have a deep faith for the Lord, he will be the one that will not compromise. The God-called pastor knows that when he moves to follow his call that the Lord will meet all his needs along the way. He knows that the Lord will provide for him, and his family, the food, and roof over their heads, as needed. God will meet all this man's needs because he, through faith, and the word of God, believes what the Lord has called him to pastor that church. This is usually the small country church pastor. The God-called man that pastors this church, and still has to work. He is the man that lets God build the church, and knows it is not his power that is doing it.

The man that is appointed by men, or the man that is not a God-called pastor but, just decides that he wants to be a pastor, has his mind focused on building a large church. He wants to get to that multi-million-dollar budget, with thousands of dollars a week coming in, he is that man that truly believes it is his job to build God's church.

The man that is man-called or appointed, and not God-called is the man that before he moves to pastor a church, has his salary already planned out, and guaranteed. His housing is secured, his car payments, and moving expenses are already covered. This is the man that when he gets to the church, will compromise on the old paths the Lord has told us to seek.

This is the man, called by men, that will soften up the preaching so it is not "offensive" to others, especially those that place large amounts of money in the offering plate. This is the man that when the going gets tough will say. "It is God's will for me to move to another church." This is an hireling, and not a God-called man that has become a pastor.

The latter man- called man, appears to be what the pastorate is all about today. The call is no longer, "How can I serve God and the people as a pastor of this church that God called me to?" The call is now. " What can God, and the church do for me before I come, and bless them with my man-made abilities that will "grow the church" like never before?" The hireling is in it for himself, the man of God is in it for the Lord.

The difference is, the God-called man will not compromise the word of God even if everyone leaves.

He will understand that the call to ministry is from God. He understands that it is God that will make a way for him to succeed, it is God that will provide true growth, it is God that brings people to the church and keeps them. The hireling will not care about spiritual growth, he will only care about his salary, and putting butts in the seats, for a "religious experience"

A God-called man will disciple the people that God has given him to shepherd. He will direct them to God in all things. He will encourage them to be in their bibles. He is the pastor that will see God change the lives of the people he is called to shepherd. The God-called pastor will see how his flock grows in their walk with God, how they are more faithful now than ever, how they will stay in the church through thick and thin, and if they have issues in the church, they will work it out and not leave.

A man-pleasing pastor will not care about discipleship. The hireling will allow others to come into the church, and work in the ministry. They appoint people to places of leadership to make them feel good, and important about themselves. They will almost never discuss salvation, and very little is said about the need to be in the bible. The sheep the man-pleasing pastor leads will be the ones that leave the moment they get their feelings hurt. These sheep will go to church, and leave in the same condition spiritually in which they came. These poor sheep will never feel that Holy Ghost conviction for sins as the pastor is not seeking that for himself. This is the church that has thousands coming in every week, but they are all babies in Christ, if they are saved at all. Many of these man-pleasing pastors are not even saved themselves.

“Pastor Chris, that is a hard statement.” Well, if they do not believe the bible for what it says then, how can they believe in the Lord Jesus Christ to be saved because that is in the bible they don’t believe themselves? But that discussion is for another time. The man-pleasing pastor will seek for and get physical results only. The God-called pastor will seek for and get spiritual results which will turn into physical results. We will discuss it later in this chapter.

Understanding the call of God on one's life to be a pastor must be achieved by one seeking God with all the heart. Every time they sit in a church service, they have feelings of needing to be doing the preaching, they have thoughts of the pastor asking them to fill in for him, or they long for the time they can preach in the youth group or children’s group. As for me, I started out preaching to children in the Junior church program at our church. I did this for many years, then I became youth director and began to teach and preach there as well.

That burden and godly desire to preach, will be on one’s mind all the time. Especially if God is asking the God-called man to take the next step. The first step in finding out if you are called to preach is to be fully surrendered to the Lord. Your heart says. “ Ok Lord, whatever, wherever, and whenever I will go” Surrendering to preach does not always mean you will be the pastor of a church. Maybe the Lord wants you to be a missionary, an evangelist, a chaplain. There are many different areas for preaching, but being fully surrendered to the call is the first thing. This is called obedience.

Many will tell you, "You must go to bible college." I will tell you that you do not have to go to Bible college. Going to Bible college is a tool that will help, and it is recommended, but the bible tells us that the bible itself is a living book inspired by God, and we are able to understand it through the Holy Ghost dwelling in us. The teaching of the Holy Ghost my dear friend, is something that colleges cannot teach you. Man-made church systems will say you must have a degree from an "accredited" college. I say how dare man put man-made restrictions on a God-called pastor.

If you truly think about it, a college is about paying them money to make you read and study the bible and other books. The college makes you pay for the books and education. If you were disciplined enough, you could read and study them on your own without you paying someone to make you do it.

I am not against colleges in any way, there is value in them. I am against however, the mindset that says if you are going to be a pastor then you must go to college first. Nowhere in the bible does it say that. The people in the bible got their teaching from the word of God. The disciples were with Jesus for three years working for the Lord, and listening to the words of the Lord. Well my dear friend, unlike the disciples in the bible, we have the completed bible in our hands today. If we just discipline ourselves enough we can search, and find the truths of the bible, and be very successful in the things of God.

A pastor without a cemetery (seminary) degree will most likely end up in a small church that may be seeking the things of God because they will not have the requirements for a pastor to be educated by knowledgeable men that must put their approval on them before they can step behind the pulpit. Many churches looking for pastors will only accept resumes from pastors with master's degrees or doctorates. It is a sad day when we have gotten to the point that we have commercialized the God-called pastorate to a man-made business system.

I have a bachelor's degree in ministry. I received it through a college by mail. My college courses were accomplished by reading commentaries on books of the bible, answering questions, and doing a test on the commentaries to get my grade. As I was going through these courses, the Holy Spirit began to reveal a question to me. Why was I reading, and studying commentaries which are man-made opinions of the word of God to get my doctrine, and not the bible itself? I said. "Well Lord, I don't know."

In the past I used commentaries to do sermon prep. After the Lord asked me that question I began to be convicted about that practice. I realized that my call to ministry was to preach the word of God, and not other men's words about God. I did finish up my courses because it was something I started, and needed to finish, but nowhere in the bible is bible college, a requirement to be a pastor. All one must do is believe the bible for what it says, be surrendered to the will of God, have a burdened heart for people, and let the Lord do what he is going to do.

When a preaching opportunity comes up, take it. Get the practice in, and let the Lord lead you. If there are not many opportunities for a person that believes that God has called them to preach, then go to the pastor and inquire about starting a nursing home ministry. If your church already has a nursing home ministry, then go to that ministry leader, and tell them you believe that God is calling you to preach. I'm sure the leader will give you opportunities to preach. This is good practice, this is letting God show you through his word what he has for you to do.

One good thing about preaching in the nursing home ministry is that they don't care if you mess up, they don't care if you are not perfect. Those seniors just want to hear something from the bible. When I worked in nursing home ministries, I preached like I do at church. I praised God for the opportunities to do what the Lord had called me to do. Plus if you really want to step up that call to ministry, don't just stop at preaching, at the nursing home, go make visits to folks. Learn how to listen, and not speak so much. Minister to the folks there, and see what God does with that call on your life.

The call to ministry is not one to be taken lightly, remember all you see in your church is that happy smiling side of your pastor, you rarely see the tears that he sheds, the broken heart that he must endure, the suffering that comes with the ministry. The pastor must go through all this, there will be seasons in ministry that are smooth, and sweet. There are also seasons that will be rough and rocky. The God-called man must hold the course, and endure the hardships then you begin to understand that call.

Being able to hold the course and enduring the hardships only comes from being in the bible, not in commentaries about the bible. The bible itself is where the true power is, as it is the inspired word of God. Commentaries are good resources, they can help you get through the hard parts, and help you to understand in the bible as you can see the different opinions of other men of God. It is essential to let the

Lord lead to the correct answer for you. I write commentaries in my “Us Common Folks” series, I make mine simple and easy to read, however I also put a warning on them not to be used as a replacement for the bible. Do not take what I am saying, even in this book, at face value, but compare it to the bible and see if this is true or just a man writing a book for himself. We will now go to the bible and see what the Lord has to say about all this.

Jeremiah 3:15
And I will give you pastors according to mine heart, which shall feed you with knowledge and understanding. The first step in understanding the call to be a pastor is that the call must come from God. In this verse God himself says that HE (not man), but HE will give you (the people) pastors AFTER his OWN heart. He did not say I will give you a man that wants to be a pastor because it seems ok to do, or one that wants a large salary. He did not say, I will give you a pastor to fill your church, he said he will give you pastors to FEED you with knowledge, and understanding.

For a pastor to be able to feed the sheep he must eat that same food, and make sure the food is the right food for his sheep. This simply means that the pastor is to be in the word. The bible must convict the pastor’s heart before it can convict the person listening to him preaching what God has placed on his heart. The pastor must meditate on the bible, seek God on it, and go to God in prayer first over what he preaches. He must take the instruction and reproof from the bible before he can pass that food on to hls people.

A pastor that is after God's own heart is directly accountable to God for how he feeds his sheep. If that shepherd (Pastor) abandons his sheep when times get tough or when some of them try to attack him, then he was not relying on God to meet those needs, he was not relying on God to walk with him through the valley.

When a pastor that is God-called realizes that his work is of the Lord, and that his job is to feed his sheep with knowledge, and truth, it gives him a new perspective. This realization gives him a renewed vision, it gives him a broken heart for those that oppose the things of God, and especially for those that are Christians that go against the things of God. A pastor MUST be after God's own heart to be able to endure through the good and bad times. In other words, they must be God-called, or they will never be successful for the things of God.

Ephesians 4:11-12
And he gave some, apostles; and some, prophets; and some, evangelists; and some, pastors and teachers; 12. For the perfecting of the saints, for the work of the ministry, for the edifying of the body of Christ: Notice that over the course of time that God gave different ages different men of God to preach, and to teach, the bible, the word of God, to people all through the world. When I say bible, in the old times they did not have the complete bible as we do today but, they did have some of the word of God, and God gave them the words they needed at the times they needed it.

In this passage we see that HE (God) gave them (us, and all people at different times) apostles; prophets; evangelists; and pastors and teachers. Make sure to note here that pastors and teachers are talking about the same person, just two separate roles, because they are not separated by a semicolon as the rest of them are. The meaning of this passage is that God made sure that the men He called, not the men that were wanting the glory of being a pastor, not the men that required large salaries, not the men that wanted health benefits or whatnot, but he, God, gave them men that he called that surrendered to his call, and preached, and taught even when others were against them. This is a person that understands his call as a Pastor, his call is from God not from a church or another person telling him to be one.

I have heard of people stepping into the role of a pastor just because no one was there to do it. Oh, how dangerous that becomes for all involved. As the man that steps into the God-called position that God did not call into that position is now directly accountable to God, and will have to answer to God for that. Woe be to the church that allows a non-God called pastor to lead them, it is only going to end up in hurt and destruction as time goes on.

In this passage also notice the God did give certain generations certain people to preach his word, this passage also lays out the main function of these God-called men, and that is to get the saints to be in their bibles so they can live holy before God, (perfecting of the saints), so they can do what is needed in the ministry. The God-called men are guiding, discipling, loving, helping, praying for, and etc. The work of the ministry is to encourage one another, to build up each other in the body of Christ, to help each other to grow in the grace of the Lord Jesus Christ.

Notice that the job of the God-called Pastor, is not really to go knock on doors, though there is value in that, it is not to change the programs in the church, though he has liberty to do so, it is not to clean the church, though he should be willing to do so, it is not to do the maintenance work at the church, though he can, it is not even to stand on the corner of the street to preach at people, though he can. The God-called pastor's job it is to teach and train the saints, those that are saved, those that are in his church congregation.

His call is to preach the truth to his people, it is to labor for them in prayer, it is to put the work in with the Lord for their interest, for them to come to him. It is a labor of love that includes hardships, hurts, frustrations, and loving no matter what. The man-pleasing pastor, or as my pastor used to say a "momma called, poppa sent pastor" will never handle the frustrations that come with loving others, the way God loves them.

Jeremiah 2:8
The priests said not, Where is the Lord? and they that handle the law knew me not: the pastors also transgressed against me, and the prophets prophesied by Baal, and walked after things that do not profit. Now we shift some to the man-pleasing pastor or even the God-called pastor that has lost his love for the Lord or has lost his vision.

Back in the day, in times past, man-pleasing pastors were few and far between. Today in the United States of America, they are everywhere, and especially in our bible believing churches. Oh man! Oh man! How we have a fight on our hands, and battles to walk through as God-called pastors. This is a job where you have no friends, it is a job that makes you angry at times, it is a job that breaks your heart. You must be resolved, to seek God, and let him guide you through the storms of these troubles.

This verse is for the man-pleasing pastor who is in the ministry for the money, the glamor, the prestige of the pastorate, the things that do NOT profit. These man-called pastors will transgress against the Lord. Transgress simply defined is: *to violate a command or law*. These pastors that are not in it for God will transgress against the things of God in favor of the things of themselves. They will focus on what they can do for themselves and if things get really messed up, they can just move to the next church down the line.

Oh how nice the ministry would be if it was sunshine, and roses all the time! Oh how nice it would be if we could preach from the heart, and thousands come to Christ every service. However, the truth is, that very few come to the Lord, very few make the changes in their lives that God asks them to make, and very few stay the course.

The pastors in this verse went against the things of God. You don't just have to go against the things of God to transgress against God. All you have to do is <u>not do</u> what he wants for you to do. That includes the modern-day pastor that is not God-called. If a pastor is not God called, they will transgress against God, and seek things that are not profitable to the Lord.

Jeremiah 10:21
For the pastors are become brutish, and have not sought the Lord: therefore they shall not prosper, and all their flocks shall be scattered. One of the

definitions of brutish simply defined is: *cruel, savage*. The pastors in the bible times, even as some are in today's times, were cruel. These pastors were acting like beasts, they would seek after the things of the world, and not care about anyone, or anything but themselves.

The Lord said that the flocks of these pastors would be scattered. There would be no peace in the churches, no growth, they would not prosper. Prosper simply defined is: *to become strong and flourishing*. They will not be strong in the Lord, and the enemy will walk all over them. My dear pastor friend, it is crucial that you continue seeking the Lord, not man-written books about the Lord. Continue to seek the bible, not man-written books about the bible, but the bible itself. Be in prayer, seek the Lord first with all your heart, and you, my friend, will then begin to move forward. There will be times of joy, and of sorrow but if you are walking in the Lord, and you understand your call, the Lord will guide you all the way. Many pastors today are brutish and have scattered God's flocks.

Jeremiah 12:10-11
Many pastors have destroyed my vineyard, they have trodden my portion under foot, they have made my pleasant portion a desolate wilderness.
11. They have made it desolate, and being desolate it mourneth unto me; the whole land is made desolate, because no man layeth it to heart.
When a pastor that is not a God-called pastor but instead is a "momma called, pappa sent pastor," they destroy the vineyard of the Lord, they destroy what the Lord is building. If they are not God called they can never lead God's people to the Lord.

The man-pleasing pastors will always be serving themselves, they will always be looking for bigger, and better churches to pastor. They will always be looking for the easy way, and they will always seek out retirement, and an easy lifestyle. If you are focused on yourself, the church will fail and will never come to the Lord. If you are focused on the Lord, and are truly God-called, then your emphasis will be on the things of God, you won't care what you get out of it, but what you can give to the Lord.

It is non-God-called men, and women today that are destroying the vineyards of the Lord. They are making a mockery of the Lord, and the bible. Once they doubt the bible for what it says, they no longer believe it, and then anything goes. God, have mercy on the souls of those that scatter the flock of God. When a person is doing ministry only for themselves God will judge them for it. Oh, how they often forget, that they too will stand before the God of Heaven and Jesus Christ, and give an answer for making people feel good about themselves. These deceivers make people think they are going to heaven instead, they are all waking up in hell being in torments.

People it is time we get back to the bible, back to the Lord, stop scattering his flock. If a person is in a pastorate that is not God-called, they need to immediately get out. The longer they are in a non-God-called position, the longer they are leading people away from the Lord. The Lord will judge a person for leading people away from him.

When we have churches today that are making homosexual people pastors, that are allowing women to be pastors, (the bible is clear that women are NOT to usurp authority over the man) that are making people feel a good experience, but they are intentionally neglecting and rejecting the truth of the bible, these non-God-called preachers have scattered the flock of God.

If I went in to preach at many churches that "believe the bible" and preached the truth of the bible as I do now, I would be kicked out of these churches faster than the speed of light. If people are not comfortable with the truth being preached, they will either repent, and get back to God, or they rebel, and run from God.

Non-God called pastors of today have made the church desolate. Yes, they have thousands coming to services, large campuses, they have their coffee shops, gossip classes, they have all the nice things, but they are lost as can be and they are not taught to seek the Lord. These poor sheep are not taught to search the bible for itself, they are not led to the Lord, only to their emotions. Many of them do not even bring their bibles to church anymore.

I have seen the posts of pastors of small churches' websites. I see all these pastors looking for dynamic programs that can motivate the people. They are looking for sermon series that are "great" and "moving people." These pastors are looking for sermon outlines, and sermons that someone else preached so they can preach the same thing in their churches. Here is why all this garbage does not work my friend, because the power of the Lord is ONLY through the bible.

When these people ask for all this stuff or what programs I use, I tell them my old King James Bible ONLY. I use no other source as the Bible is inspired by God, it is quick and powerful, it is complete, throughly furnished to do the job. It is the words of God, backed by the Holy Spirit. This is a position they reject as they believe the way of the old timers does not work. It is funny when I hear them say that the old ways of doing things do not work for today's church. I read in my bible Jeremiah 6:16 where the Lord says SEEK the OLD paths which are the GOOD ways, I must ask myself in that moment, do I believe the bible or man?

My dear pastor friend, if you are one of these pastors leading God's sheep away from him, try turning to the bible and see what happens. If you are not God-called then resign, and let a God-called man get in there for the sake of the church. Churches today do not care if the man in the pulpit is God called or not. All they are looking for is an employee to run their programs, a man they can control. It is the man of God, called by God, that puts all that nonsense to rest, and leads people to God.

Jeremiah 17:16-17
As for me, I have not hastened from being a pastor to follow thee: neither have I desired the woeful day; thou knowest: that which came out of my lips was right before thee. 17. Be not a terror unto me: thou art my hope in the day of evil. The prophet Jeremiah tells the Lord that he has not quit the work of the Lord, he has not stopped from being a pastor, he has not led people away from the things of the Lord.

He goes on to say the words that came out of his mouth were right before the Lord. He spoke the truth of the word of God, he spoke it to help all who would receive it. He spoke it under the threat of persecution, he was truly a God-called man because he stood the test of time, he stood the battles, he held his course, he kept the faith, he endured, he did not leave but he clave to the things of God. God is our hope in the day of evil.

Folks, pastors, we are in the day of evil now! Is the Lord enough for you, are you a truly God-called pastor that is looking out for others? Are you a truly God-called pastor that is seeking God through the bible, and not other books? I am not against other books as this is the thirteenth one I have written, there is a vast world of knowledge in books, it is just that men have been taught today that being a pastor you must refer to the manmade resources to validate the word of God, and that is not what the Lord said to do.

We are to STUDY to shew ourselves approved unto God. We are to study the bible, and use all the other books as resources comparing them against the bible not comparing the bible against them. Get back to the OLD paths my dear pastor friend, and see what God can do.

Jeremiah 22:22
The wind shall eat up all thy pastors, and thy lovers shall go into captivity: surely then shalt thou be ashamed and confounded for all thy wickedness. Pastors who are not God-called will drive the sheep aways from the great Shepherd. If these men are not God-called then they are man-pleasing, and they will blow in and out of ministries like the wind. There will be no meat for their congregations, they will not produce any fruit, and they will run when the going gets tough.

These man-pleasing pastors are destroying churches these days as they make ministry all about themselves, their money, and large fancy services designed to produce a religious experience that has no conviction or Holy Spirit power behind it. These are the pastors that go to others and not the bible for their messages. These are pastors that must have programs, and not preaching. These are pastors that are eaten up by the wind.

Jeremiah 23:1-4

Woe be unto the pastors that destroy and scatter the sheep of my pasture! saith the Lord. Woe simply defined is: *an expression of grief, regret, or distress*. The bible tells us here that there will come regret, distress, and grief for the PASTORS that scatter the sheep of the Lord. If a person is not seeking the Lord they are drifting away from him. All a man-pleasing pastor can ever do is scatter the sheep of the Lord, as the Lord is not behind his calling. How can the man-called pastor lead people to seek the Lord through the power of the Holy Spirit when he himself is not seeking that power? How can he show people the power of faith, and endurance when he himself is leaving the church because of every bad look that someone gives him? The pastors that are man-pleasing will lead the sheep away from God, and closer to the systems of the world.

For the pastor that is God-called, woe to him even more as he knows better, if he falls into that prideful sin. Pastors are easily faced daily, with that monster called pride. After a church service, especially one where the Holy Spirit showed up and a person says, “Pastor, that was a great message.” that pride monster is whispering in your ear. “Yes it was, you did that good message.”

God-called Pastors are men with sin natures and can be drawn away of their own lust if they are not in the bible, and in prayer every day. The God-called pastor must be intentional about their walk with God, or they will drive away and scatter the sheep of the Lord. Woe be to them that make a mockery, or make a commercial job, out of the ministry. Ministry is about living by faith, seeking the Lord's call, and clinging to him. A truly God-called pastor that is seeking God will cleave to his ministry and not leave his ministry.

2. Therefore thus saith the Lord God of Israel against the pastors that feed my people; Ye have scattered my flock, and driven them away, and have not visited them: behold, I will visit upon you the evil of your doings, saith the Lord. Very strong warnings from the Lord. God will visit the sin, the evil of their doings, of the pastors upon them, this means that their congregations will suffer right along with them. The things they try and do will fail, there will be a lack of peace, there will be distress in the ministry, and the Lord holds that pastor accountable for what they do.

I mentioned earlier in the book that whoever fills the position of the pastor, whether they are God or man called, whether gay, or straight, male or female, they will be held accountable for that position of a pastor. This is above and beyond any other sins they are living in or are accountable for as the Lord says he will visit the evil of their doings upon them. When you think about that for a moment, you can understand why the hireling (man-pleasing pastor) runs, and leaves when things get tough. They are beginning to be held accountable; they are beginning to have their evil visited upon them for the ministry they are leading. If the pastor is not leading their ministry to the Lord they are leading them to the world, there are no other options.

The call of God MUST be on a pastor for him to do the work God has in store for him. If he is following that call God will make a way for that call to happen. God will make a way for him to hold the course. The difference between God-called, and man-pleasing is that God-called pastors have the backing of the Lord behind them, whereas the man-pleasing only has his own efforts backing them. Folks, we must do things God's way, we are in too great a battle against sin to allow the enemy to attack us from within the church.

3 And I will gather the remnant of my flock out of all countries whither I have driven them, and will bring them again to their folds; and they shall be fruitful and increase. 4 And I will set up shepherds over them which shall feed them: and they shall fear no more, nor be dismayed, neither shall they be lacking, saith the Lord. The Lord says that after the sheep are scattered, and the evil is visited upon the people, that he will gather them again, and place shepherds over them.

Think about this verse for a moment, and all of the small pastor less churches out there. Do you suppose that at one time they had their evil visited upon them? Do you suppose that at one time they had pastors that were not God-called, or they were God-called and the man gave into the temptations of his sin and that evil was visited upon their church?

Today there is a statement going around that a church is "dying," that the church as a whole will be dead in a few years. Well my friend, according to this verse all churches that are God-centered can be restored by allowing God to put the pastor in the pulpit. Once the Lord places that God-called pastor in that church that church can then be restored, it can be revitalized, it can draw closer to God. I am not in favor of closing any bible-based church, but the churches need to remove the educational, experience, and other man-restrictions on the position of pastor and accept a pastor by the fruits of his life, and his walk with the Lord, and let God restore his church. That is my opinion.

Nehemiah 1:8-9
Remember, I beseech thee, the word that thou commandedst thy servant Moses, saying, If ye transgress, I will scatter you abroad among the nations: 9. But if ye turn unto me, and keep my commandments, and do them; though there were of you cast out unto the uttermost part of the heaven, yet will I gather them from thence, and will bring them unto the place that I have chosen to set my name there. This passage here is simply saying that no matter how far scattered a person, a church, or nation may be, if they turn back to God, he can restore them.

As a God-called Pastor the goal is to get the people back to God. It is to teach them how to seek God with all their hearts, minds, and souls and let God change their lives through the word of God. One must be in their bible to do this. It is not up to the lost of the world to come to the church so it can grow, it is for the saved, those that are children of God to repent, and turn back to God. A God-called pastor knows this because this is his primary focus

A God-called pastor knows that he must labour in prayer, fasting, visiting, building relationships to get the people to see Jesus, and for them to see how God works. It is encouraging for those in the church when you pray for something and God answers that prayer and then you point out that God did answer that prayer. We serve a big God who wants to meet all our needs, and not only that, he wants to give us the best of what he has. God is able, willing, and ready to do exceedingly abundantly above all we could ask or think (Ephesians 3:20). If God is that willing, and you are not receiving, then you must ask, why?

I had to ask myself, why haven't I seen the power that Elijah had in the bible? Why haven't I gotten the rewards that were given to men, and women in the service of the Lord? Well, the Lord had to convict my heart, and remind me that he is the same yesterday, today, and forever, and that if there is a gap in our relationship that gap was on me, and not on him. I am diligently seeking that power, and faith from the bible. Nowhere in the bible does it say that God cannot still give that Holy Ghost power today. There is just too much sin, and the weights that so easily beset us in our lives for us to see, or allow these blessings to happen.

My dear pastor friend, if you are a truly God-called pastor, then pastor your church. If God calls you to a church with six people, pastor them like it is the most important thing for you to do. Love them. It is God's job and responsibility to build his church. The bible is clear about that. We are shown over and over again, it is the job of the pastor to preach, and teach no matter the state of life they are in, good, bad, or otherwise.

Oh, this is not the same for the man-called man who wants to pastor then retire or jump from ministry to ministry. I heard a pastor one time say that he had pastored for twenty years in nine different churches. This pastor said it as though it was something to be proud of. Think about that. That is a new church nearly every two years. That short amount of time is not enough to endure hardships, it is not enough to hold the course, it is not enough to see what you can endure as a God-called pastor. It is only the hireling that will jump ship when the going gets tough. The hireling will look for that retirement, or big paycheck when they are serving. What is your call my dear friend? Is it the call of God or man?

John 15:16-19
Ye have not chosen me, but I have chosen you, and ordained you, that ye should go and bring forth fruit, and that your fruit should remain: that whatsoever ye shall ask of the Father in my name, he may give it you. This is the simplest verse in the bible as far as the call of God on one to preach or teach. It is simply God that calls, and if God calls he will make it happen.

My dear friend, the time is now here when the world will not endure sound doctrine, (II Timothy 4:3) but God will get you through that. If you are a God-called pastor it is because God has called you to get through it. You surrendered to do his will, therefore he will make a way for it to happen. The problem with pastors today is they want the type of church like it was back in the forties, fifties, and sixties. It was a time where people knew they had to be in church, where they would come out of respect, out of the fear of God and out of obligation. The churches would be full and the God called man could preach anything, and everything in the bible. You could yell at people from the pulpit, and they would listen. If they did get their feelings hurt they would come back the next time, and endure it again.

Those days are gone. Now we are the pastors that must preach knowing that the day has come when people will not endure this sound doctrine. What does that tell a person when the pastor himself will not even endure sound doctrine? It shows that they were not in it for the Lord but, for themselves. When you endure the hardships there is ALWAYS victory after the hardship. If you endure, the Lord will bring more people in.

If the Lord allowed you to pastor a church with two hundred people, a full-time salary, and benefits, (again nothing wrong with that, as long as it is not the main focus) and you have not learned to endure through the hard times, then how will you ever hold the course? It is great to start out in churches with five or six people attending, the pastor can build from there. Let me tell you, even a church running about twenty can be hard because you are still dealing with people that have sin natures, and many are babes in Christ. When God called you he ordained you to go and bring forth fruit, and that fruit should remain.

17. These things I command you, that ye love one another. 18. If the world hate you, ye know that it hated me before it hated you. 19. If ye were of the world, the world would love his own: but because ye are not of the world, but I have chosen you out of the world, therefore the world hateth you. This is almost a sucker punch for that non-God-called pastor, the non-God-called pastor will not want to be hated by people, and yes, my friend, people in the ministry will hate you at times. Yes my friend, those that say they are saved will hate you at times, especially if they are in that carnal state of mind.

People hate the truth and they hate the person delivering that truth even more because they can then see, and hear that truth. If the truth is only in the bible, and they keep their bibles shut they can ignore that truth and live how they want. If the pastor is preaching against their sin they will hate him. Go to any of these compromising bible-denying churches that have high attendance and multi-campuses and listen to the preaching. At these churches you will only hear the neutral stuff being preached. You will only hear the stuff that makes a person feel good about themselves, and nothing about turning from their sin. Take that same church and those same campuses and begin to preach the truth of the bible for what it says, start preaching against fornication, drinking, cursing, adultery and see how much that church reduces in size and income over the next few months. See how in the next year or so that church is selling some of those other campuses, how the pastoral staff has left, and how the church has dwindled. In reality that would not happen, because in these non-biblical, board led churches, the board members would be the ones offended, and they would fire that pastor. Oh! how the people hate the truth.

When I was on my road to repentance, which was not an easy road for me to be on, there were a lot of uncomfortable adjustments that I had to make in my life. I had many times of frustration, especially in the beginning, there were many times I wanted to quit, but the Lord put a friend in my life at that time that told me something that has stuck with me through this journey. My friend said, "If ministry was easy anyone could do it however, God has chosen you to do it." This simply means that God has called me to it, I will do it, and let the results be up to God. God will make it happen.

JUST BECAUSE YOU CAN

Matthew 24:5
For many shall come in my name, saying, I am Christ; and shall deceive many.

Just because you can does not mean that you should. How many times in life do you hear someone say, "Well I'll do it, just because I can." Lately I have been watching videos that people have been putting on YouTube about interactions with the police, and the situations they get themselves into. Though I strongly believe in police accountability, and that there are many police in the United States that abuse the power they have, and get away with it, there are way more honest people trying to make a difference in their societies. My son is a Sheriff deputy in Florida, so I understand that cops overall are good, it is the bad ones that put a black mark for all of them.

I used this illustration to say that in the case of folks that have those interactions with the police, some of them are making fools of themselves just trying to carry their guns around, and wearing masks out in public just because they can. I support the constitution and I enjoy the benefits of our amendments (though some are not biblically based.)

In certain circumstances, these constitutional auditors, as they call themselves, should not be so blunt with their displays. Many of these displays cause them to be arrested, and in some things they are wrong. Their display causes them to have criminal records and hardships. Sometimes just because you can do it, does not mean that you should.

You can jump out of an airplane without a parachute, but you probably should not as the end of the trip there will be destruction. This is no different in the pastorate, there are many people who have a gift of teaching, but no business pastoring. There are some that can preach very well, but should not be pastoring. Evangelists are preachers, but they are not pastors. If a person's calling is not for pastoring they should refrain from doing it as all they are going to end up doing is making a bad mark for the things of God. There will be no power in the church, and that church will restrain God from doing what he wants to do.

This is one pressure that evangelists and missionaries face as they travel to preach or raise support. When they visit these local churches that need pastors to present their work, these churches have been without a pastor for so long that an evangelist comes in and they get a breath of refreshment, and then they want that evangelist to come and be their pastor. I have heard many testimonies of how people that were pastors, some even for years, are now in evangelism, because that was the calling of God for them. They realized that just because they were able to fill that pulpit on a permanent basis it did not mean that they should have.

The pastorate is a sacred place. If a person is in that position they are held accountable for that position. If they are saved, love the Lord, can preach, but not called, then all they are is a false shepherd that is leading the sheep away from God and the greatness that the Lord has to offer. These will be the pastors that know, at times, that they may not be called by God but they do not want to disappoint the people in the church so they remain for a while.

These are the pastors that pastor churches and long for retirement from preaching as that is the noble way out of service for the Lord. Retirement will enable them to say they did not quit. Again these are not bad people, nor do I necessarily believe they are living in sin. I just believe that if they are not called by God they have no business as a pastor as the best they can do is lead people to themselves and away from the things of God. If a person does take a pulpit and they are not a God-called Pastor that should be for a set amount of time to help the church get by until a God-called pastor can be provided by the Lord.

I'm sure over the course of one's call into ministry a man may question their calling into that ministry. In their heart, they know the calling is from the Lord, they also know if they are not called of God as well. They may try to hang in there for a while but my friend, if a man is not a God-called pastor, he will not put in a God-called effort into this ministry, he will not be invested with ALL his heart, mind, and soul.

How sad a day it will be when that person stands before the Lord, knowing that they were not a God-called pastor. They find out that if they had just stepped down and did what the Lord had for them to do, that many souls would be credited to their ministry. Again, the person that is a pastor simply because he can be, knows it. If he is truly seeking God with all his heart, mind and soul, he will have conviction from the Lord about stopping what he is doing.

I understand, as do many, that it is good to feel needed and to be able to help out a church, or even be the “hero” for a church that is in dire need. The non-God-called pastor may even be convinced that if he does not take the pulpit, that the church of many years will be forced to close. I get that, but let me ask an earlier question again. Whose church is this? Is it your church or God’s church? If it is God’s church then he, not you, will fill that need. God knows the needs of every one of his churches and is making a way for those needs to be met. So, if you are not called by God then do yourself a favor in your walk with God and do NOT take the pulpit just because you can because that will be another black mark for churches, and pastors. The church led by a man-called pastor will be a weight in that person’s life and the pastor will in actuality be rebelling against the call that God does have on their life.

God has placed a call on each and every believer. That call is for them to be found by living for the Lord. The Lord will direct you to the calling that he has for you. For example, a person that has a gift of teaching, and can bring a preaching message, maybe God has called that person to be a professor at a bible college, or a bible teacher in the local Christian high school. Their part in ministry can be laying up treasures in heaven for the future generations. Maybe, just maybe, if that person that is not called by God to preach fills the role of a pastor just because he can, he will miss out on that treasure from teaching in that local school.

If that is his true calling, his joy will be filled. Do it God's way, and let him deal with the rest.

If more people, and pastors, lived by faith alone in the God of the bible, we would see more God-called pastors filling his pulpits, and see more people come back to God. After a while the man that is pastoring just because he can, and is not God-called, will begin to become numb to that conviction of the Holy Spirit in his life. There will be very little, if any, fruit from them or the ministry that they have chosen. The bible says by their fruits you shall know them.

Seeing a man's fruit is the biggest thing to prove whether a man is a false prophet or a God called prophet. If a man is a false prophet, or doing it just because they can do it, you will see that in the fruits that are produced from the ministry. If they are God-called and truly seeking him you will see those fruits as well. Time to go to the bible to see what it says. Once again, just because you can, does not mean you should, and most likely you probably should not.

Matthew 7:15-20
Beware of false prophets, which come to you in sheep's clothing, but inwardly they are ravening wolves. 16. Ye shall know them by their fruits. Do men gather grapes of thorns, or figs of thistles?
There are so many false teachers, and preachers out there today that we must diligently be in the truth of the bible to be able to spot them, and call them out as needed. Knowing the truth of the bible, and the bible only, will allow you to defend anything that comes along that is not bible.

I truly believe it is because of rebellion that we have so many churches out there today of different denominations, and religious beliefs. I also believe that it is because of the rebellion against the truth of the bible that we have people just stepping into these church leadership roles as pastors, and scattering the sheep away from the Lord.

When I say rebellion I am simply saying that people have rebelled against the truth of the bible over the years. Pastors who are not God-called, but man-pleasing have rebelled against God because they are doing something they have no business doing. They are disguising themselves as pastors doing ministry for the Lord, but if they are saved, they truly know they are disguising themselves because the conviction of the Holy Ghost will be there as well.

It is simple, you either believe the bible for what it says, or you do not. There are many, a large majority of people that have chosen not to believe the bible for what it says and have become false prophets. These false prophets will come disguised as godly people, they will have a form of godliness, but they will deny that power thereof. These false prophets will make you feel all warm and fuzzy inside, but there will be no Holy Ghost power in them, or in what they do.

A person that is pastoring just because he can, will have very little, or no fruit for the Lord. Now, to be clear on what I am saying here. I said no fruit for the Lord. Yes, they may get thousands of people coming to church, they may be able to manage five campuses for their churches. But, how many of those people are these false prophets actually leading to Christ? If you could put a percentage on it, probably five to ten percent will be truly seeking God, maybe.

It is these non-God called men and women standing behind the pulpit that will produce earthly fruit that will be mistaken for heavenly fruit. Their ministry will be filled with people that come to church, leave just as lost, as un-convicted, as non-receptive, and just as bible rejecting as when they walked in the door. Their fruit will be reflected in the ministry. On a side note, women pastors are non-biblical pastors. The bible forbids women from taking the pulpit as pastors. (I Timothy 2:12)

Oh my dear pastor friend, it is about the Holy Ghost conviction that only the Lord can bring in a person's life. If you are truly preaching the bible for what it says, people will hate you, they will fight with you, they will curse you. The bible tells us that people will hate us because they first hated Jesus, and when we get right down to it, we are preaching the same message that Jesus preached. They hated the truth then, and my dear friend, they still hate that truth. Do the fruits that come from you show the glory of a God called pastor, or do they show the world fruits of a man-called pastor who has no business in the pulpit, but is doing it just because he can?

17. Even so every good tree bringeth forth good fruit; but a corrupt tree bringeth forth evil fruit. If the person that is pastoring is not a God-called pastor all he can ever do is produce corrupt fruit. This is the reason we have so many false religions out there today. I am not trying to be mean, I am just saying what the bible says. If you are a God-called pastor you will be seeking God with all your heart, mind, and soul and you will produce fruit that will last for the Lord, and not produce corrupt fruit.

Corrupt simply defined is: *to change from good to bad*. WOW think about that, changing the message of the bible from good to bad. The bible tells us in Romans that people will change the truth of God into a lie and they will worship and serve the creature more than the creator. How does this truth get changed from good to bad? It is changed by the pastors being corrupt. A corrupt pastor is a non-God-called pastor, who will corrupt the truth of the bible as he is not seeking that truth himself. If the pastor was seeking that truth for himself he would resign his position, and do what the Lord has asked him to do instead of doing this just because he can. It takes a real man to repent and to truly seek the call that God has on one's life. Are you guilty of corrupting the bible?

Women pastors from the very start, are corrupting the bible. Yes, they are "pastoring" just because they can, but they are pastoring out of a rebellion to the bible therefore, everything they base their belief on will also be in rebellion against the bible. It is impossible for a person to say they believe the bible while living in sin against the bible. If a woman is pastoring she is automatically in rebellion to the word of God. If she says she believes the bible, then it is only because she is selective on what she does and does not believe. You must either believe the whole bible for what it says, or you must reject it all for what it says. If you deny some of the bible you must deny it all, because it is a Holy Bible and if you reject some of it, then how can you say it is Holy?

People pastoring just because they can are corrupters that are bringing forth corrupt fruit. Bringing forth corrupt fruit means you are producing worldly fruit that rejects God in some areas of your life. I do find it interesting though that there is one biblical principle all religions believe. They all believe the part in the bible in Malachi that says bring your tithes to the store house, you can be assured that every church believes in that.

The battle for the Lord is tough enough without having to fight corruption from within. Satan loves the fact that God's people are fighting with each other. It gets God's people off the battlefield and away from God as they run to the side of Satan which is disguised as new and better. Oh Lord have mercy on the souls that lead your sheep astray and scatter them abroad.

18. A good tree cannot bring forth evil fruit, neither can a corrupt tree bring forth good fruit. A God-called pastor will not produce corrupt fruit. He will hold the course, he will be in the bible, he will seek the Lord, he will endure the test of time, he will live what he believes and he will rejoice in the Lord even if no one comes. The God called man will preach the truth, he will not compromise, he will direct each, and every person to the Lord, and to the bible for all their answers.

The God called man will not direct the sheep to himself, or to the denomination, he will make it all about the Lord. The God called man will preach his heart out every week, he will labour in prayer each and every day for the sheep that have been entrusted to him, he will weep for them at times, he will hurt when they hurt, he will love when they love, he will be a parent to them when needed, a friend, a counselor. I will say one hundred percent for sure that a man-pleasing pastor will tuck tail and run when the going gets tough in his ministry. In contrast, the truly God-called pastor will hold the course no matter the situation.

19. Every tree that bringeth not forth good fruit is hewn down, and cast into the fire. There are trees that are struck by lightning, and some don't get the correct water they need. These trees become corrupt. I have seen trees in Florida where I grew up that had fungus on them. If that fungus was not treated then it would take over that tree, and that tree would begin to die. The tree would become a corrupt tree.

This passage is saying that the person that is focused on Jesus and the bible will produce good fruit, but one that rejects the truth of the bible or the call of God on their lives they will eventually end up producing corrupt fruit. A pastor that is in the pulpit, that is not called of God, will eventually produce corrupt fruit. There can be people who have surrendered to preach and will one day, maybe become a pastor, but if it is not in God's timing the same thing will happen. The person that is truly seeking God's will and is truly called by God to be a pastor, will know when it is their time to take a ministry. It is the ones that are not called by God, or as in my case, many years ago, that are living in sin trying to force God's will, that are fruitless and corrupt. I will save that story for another format.

The Lord says that he will cast down every corrupt tree that brings forth corrupt fruit. The bible tells us in Jeremiah, as I referred to it in a previous chapter, woe to the pastors that scatter the sheep abroad, woe to the ones that are doing the work without the call. Folks that are pastoring and not called of God, can only be in the ministry for themselves. They will not live by faith or even know how to live by faith, and the bible tells us that without faith it is impossible to please God. (Hebrews 11:6) The bible also states that whatsoever is not of faith, is sin (Romans 14:23) This means the best that the man-pleasing pastor can ever do is lead people to himself which we see that a lot in the church today. Where are those old time God-believing, faith-living Christians that actually accomplished things for the Lord? They are few and far between.

20 Wherefore by their fruits ye shall know them. A person can lie about so many different things in their lives. People can put up a godly front to impress others, but sooner or later the true self will come out, it will show itself and then you will either see if they are honest or telling a lie. Lies destroy, truth strengthens. Even as bible believing pastors we are faced with the temptations of telling lies, as with all temptations. But, it is in those moments that the truth of who we are will not allow us to continue or to even start in those lies.

The fruit is what a person produces, the way a person walks for the Lord, and talks about God is what their life produces. A man-pleasing pastor will only produce surface results, and surface feelings, the best he will ever do is make people feel good about themselves. He can generate religious experiences, and motivate people to give their money to him, but he will not be able to show people what living by faith is all about, he will not be able to show people what it is like to seek God and rely on him, he will not be able to show people what it is like to be in the word of God daily and see the changes that come as a result of that walk with God. The man-called pastor does more harm than good for the cause of Christ, the man-called pastor makes a mockery of the Lord and the church and needs to step down so the Lord can restore his church. Woe to the pastors that destroy and scatter the sheep (Jeremiah 23:1)

Many people today don't read their bible. Often they will rely on the pastor for the truth of the bible. The God-called pastor will always direct that person to the bible but the man-pleasing pastor will direct them to counseling, and this, or that program, because they are not seeking the bible themselves. On the heels of Jeremiah 23:1 woe to the pastors that destroy and scatter the sheep, all that the man-called pastor filling a pulpit, and leading a church that is not supported by the power of God is going to get is woe.

The bible tells us that we cannot serve two masters. We cannot serve both God and (mammon) or man, we will hate one and love the other. If that person filling the pulpit is doing it just because they can do it then, anything goes. In today's society we now have homosexuals being called pastors, they are leading churches and counseling people. They are living in sin, and they are now leading the sheep of God? Woe to those pastors that destroy and scatter the sheep of God, all this sin in the pulpit happens because someone, not called by God, at some point, filled a pulpit just because they could fill it..

1 John 4:1-6
Beloved, believe not every spirit, but try the spirits whether they are of God: because many false prophets are gone out into the world. This is talking to those that are saved. They are to try and test the man of God, most of the time if you just sit and listen you will hear the fruits of their life showing through. One of the disconnects in today's world, and the reason so many man-pleasing pastors are out

there is because, the churches have been without pastors for so long. Many churches are only looking for CEO's for their church. These pastor less churches will accept anything or anyone that comes along to have that security.

If a person wants to be a pastor, whether God-called or man-pleasing, and wants to do it on their own, all they would have to do is find a church that has been without a pastor for a while. These churches usually have five to ten people attending. The candidate can put up a front before the people, and that man can become the pastor of that church. These false prophets will lead these churches to the methods of man and not to the faith in the Lord.

There is a movement today where man-pleasing pastors are going into these small churches, putting up a front and showing a form of godliness, and getting themselves voted into these small churches as pastors. Soon, their families come and join the church and gain the majority voting rights in that church. The majority votes to dissolve the church, sell the property and live off the money from the sale of the property. Sadly this is happening a lot. Many of these small churches, that need pastors, are able to stay afloat because they are debt free, and have only their utilities to pay for.

This is a sad day when there is corruption in the pulpit, and again, pastors need to be tried, and proven to be true. Call and check with their former churches. Do your due diligence and follow the leading of the Holy Spirit to see if they are truly God-called or man-pleasing. Just because a person can fill a pulpit does not mean they should. The ministry in itself has changed from having its focus on God to having its focus on man and that my dear pastor friend, has been our downfall.

Look at the resume of a pastor. Does it show many churches in a few years? How much time was spent at any one church? It takes about five years for a pastor to get established in a church. Many pastors today will move to new churches every two to three years, just as the going gets tough. These false prophets tend to all of a sudden feel the call to go somewhere else.

2. Hereby know ye the Spirit of God: Every spirit that confesseth that Jesus Christ is come in the flesh is of God: 3 And every spirit that confesseth not that Jesus Christ is come in the flesh is not of God: and this is that spirit of antichrist, whereof ye have heard that it should come; and even now already is it in the world. The false teaching and the anti-God mindsets of today already dominate this world. When a pastor steps behind a pulpit, they are representing God on the highest level. When that person takes over God's church they are supposed to be shepherding his sheep, they are to keep his church holy, and when they do this just because they can and not because they are called, they end up doing work for the antichrist. Satan and his army will never lead anyone to Christ nor can they as Christ and Satan are totally opposite.

The bible is clear that you cannot serve two masters, and God hates when a person is lukewarm. We must conclude that when a non-God called person is doing the work of a God-called person by just filling in because they can, they can never lead God's sheep to God. All they can ever do is lead people to themselves. If all the pastors today that are just filling in because they can, would resign their pulpits, and let the truly God-called pastors take over, there would be many liberal churches closing. There would also be many people rejecting this, but at the same time there would be much more holiness in the pulpits and people would begin to fall in love with the Lord Jesus Christ, and lives would begin to change for him.

4. Ye are of God, little children, and have overcome them: because greater is he that is in you, than he that is in the world. 5. They are of the world: therefore speak they of the world, and the world heareth them. 6. We are of God: he that knoweth God heareth us; he that is not of God heareth not us. Hereby know we the spirit of truth, and the spirit of error. When a person, or a truly God-called pastor is walking with God, you will see that in his life. It will be reflected in his preaching, his teaching, and his ministry.

The love of God will run through that God-called pastor like there is no tomorrow. The God called pastor will be the one that preaches those difficult messages that others hate because it shows them their sin. He will be that one that loves and cries for them, the one that when the church comes to him and says we have no more money to pay you, he still preaches, and teaches just as he did when he first got there, and when they were able to pay him. The reason is because he is not working for himself or the church but he is doing it for the Lord, he is doing it because he is called by God to do it, and is not doing it just because he can.

The God-called pastor has overcome all priority for the material gains for the pastorate that the man-pleasing pastor is so focused on today. Try taking away the paycheck and the house of the man-pleasing pastor and watch just how "God-called" they really are as they throw their fits, as they yell and scream, as they leave and jump ship. One thing else to be said of man-pleasing pastors is you will NEVER see them taking churches that are small in number and or one that has little to no money coming in. Why is that? Because those small churches require a pastor to live by faith, which is what the ministry is all about. However, the larger liberal churches will offer "competitive wages" as they say today.

Man-pleasing pastors do not trust that "greater is he that is in me," they do not long for or seek after the Holy Spirit's guidance. These man-pleasing pastors will compromise the bible, they will compromise the doctrines they once believed, I have even heard some of them say, "Well, I don't agree with everything the church says or believes but it is not a real big issue so I can overlook it." I say. " Yes, you can overlook it because you have no convictions, because you compromise the Holy word of God and you are willing to continue in this God-rejecting path just because you are getting a comfortable paycheck."

A man-pleasing pastor has also eliminated the being saved requirement for the pastor to fill a pulpit. If a pastor is not saved, he will never have the power of the Lord on him, or in his preaching, or in his teaching all he can ever do is lead people to himself. WOE to him when he stands before God not just as a lost sinner, but as a man that intentionally led God's sheep to the slaughter.

2 Peter 2:1-9
But there were false prophets also among the people, even as there shall be false teachers

among you, who privily shall bring in damnable heresies, even denying the Lord that bought them, and bring upon themselves swift destruction. Apparently the Lord knew about this before we did, that false doctrines and teachers would come into the churches and lead God's people astray. If you do not believe that a man-pleasing pastor is a false teacher, then my dear reader friend, I want to challenge you to search the word of God like never before, because if they are not OF God, then they are AGAINST God.

The bible tells us as Christians and the churches today that they are to beware of the false prophets. When a non-God called pastor takes over a church they are a false prophet. These men are preaching and teaching on faith when they have no idea on living it or believing it for themselves. A person can convince themselves that they are God-called, but watch, look, listen to them, time will tell. See how they react when the money is not there, when the going gets tough. Look at the average pastoral candidates resume today. You will see in a seven-to-eight-year period where they had experience as a pastor for about two years in four different churches. These men will tell you that they were able to accomplish great things and build that church. I would then ask why are you not still there enjoying the fruit that you had a part in planting?

Man-pleasing pastors are God denying pastors and they can never be truly God promoting pastors because they do not have the power of God on their ministry. Did you notice in the book of Acts, that some people only worked a job and told others about Jesus? Not everyone that got saved pastored churches. Why do you suppose that is? It is because only the God-called ones are the ones the God gave the guts to handle all the obstacles that will come in the pastorate.

God is the only one that can bring comfort to his pastor when all goes wrong, God is the only one that has given his pastor the courage to keep coming back and to keep preaching the truth especially when everyone hates that truth and hates him for preaching it. It is only God that gives the victory when that difficult time has ended, a man-pleasing, God-rejecting, pastor would have left that church high, and dry, and moved to another church

I want to take a moment here to address those small churches looking for a pastor. I understand that you are in dire need of a shepherd, that you need someone to lead your flock, but please, please, do not just take the first person that comes along just because he is there. Make sure to wait on the Lord's guidance and see if he is willing to move across the country to pastor your church for no money? That is a good sign that that person is doing this for the Lord, please, again, do not just fill your empty pulpit just because you can, but do it God's way, make the call of God a requirement and then see what God can do.

Man-pleasing pastors have no convictions in their lives, and they will begin to teach things that are opposite of faith as they themselves are not living by faith. These men pleasers will begin to teach and get the church to accept the damnable heresies that are against the Lord and against the bible. They will do it under the disguise of being put there by the Lord. If you are seeking the Lord he will give you the needed discernment to distinguish (wow another big word for me, lol) between right and wrong, between truth and damnable heresies.

2. And many shall follow their pernicious ways; by reason of whom the way of truth shall be evil spoken of. 3. And through covetousness shall they with feigned words make merchandise of you: whose judgment now of a long time lingereth not, and their damnation slumbereth not. The false prophets will speak evil of the truth, they will lead the sheep to the slaughter, they will scatter the sheep of the Lord as we saw in Jeremiah, and the payment that will be made by those non-God called pastors that lead the sheep astray, will be severe.

Notice that the bible here says, "that they will make merchandise of you." That is saying these false prophets, these non-God called pastors, will be in it for the money, they will get all the money and benefits they can from the church and from the Lord's ministry. These same people will hate guys like me who are bible believing and living on faith. They will get what they can from the church and then move onto another one, and so on, and so on. All in the name of the Lord. Yes, their churches will have thousands coming, but those same thousands are just as lost, and living in sin when they leave the church as they are when they entered that church because the Holy Spirit is not welcomed in those churches.

4. For if God spared not the angels that sinned, but cast them down to hell, and delivered them into chains of darkness, to be reserved unto judgment; 5. And spared not the old world, but saved Noah the eighth person, a preacher of righteousness, bringing in the flood upon the world of the ungodly; 6. And turning the cities of

Sodom and Gomorrha into ashes condemned them with an overthrow, making them an ensample unto those that after should live ungodly; 7. And delivered just Lot, vexed with the filthy conversation of the wicked: 8. (For that righteous man dwelling among them, in seeing and hearing, vexed his righteous soul from day to day with their unlawful deeds;) 9. The Lord knoweth how to deliver the godly out of temptations, and to reserve the unjust unto the day of judgment to be punished:

Maybe you are a God-called pastor that is struggling. Read this passage. God knows how to deliver you into his righteousness, the God-called pastor knows, and believes this even when he wants to quit, even when he is kicked, and down he knows that God will deliver him, and the ministry for which he has suffered. The man-pleasing pastor will NEVER suffer for the things of the Lord, let alone the things of the Lord's flock.

This passage says that the Lord knows how to "reserve the unjust unto the day of judgment." This means that the man-pleasing pastor may not answer to God here on this earth, he may continue to go, and take, and go, and take, from many churches, but at the judgment which all of us are appointed to, he will then have to answer for those deeds. The bible is clear my dear pastor friend, if you are a man-pleasing pastor God will reserve you to judgment before him. If you are a God-called pastor the Lord will deliver you from the situations that you are in. Keep on, keeping on, for the Lord and you will see God accomplish great things through you, but not because of you. If you are filling a pulpit and not called of God to do so, resign the pulpit, and get the peace and power of God on your life by doing what he has called you to do. Don't do something just because you can.

God or Satan

A Pastor or CEO

Matthew 6:24
No man can serve two masters: for either he will hate the one, and love the other; or else he will hold to the one, and despise the other. Ye cannot serve God and mammon.

Churches all across the United States are no longer looking for a pastor to lead them but a man that they themselves can lead. It is a common mindset that the church has a pastor to "lead" them but, these modern-day churches all have a board of directors that can hire the pastor they want in place or fire him. These pastors do not really have any authority in the church, they are to preach, and lead within guidelines set by the board. In some churches the pastor is not allowed to talk about difficult subjects, such as hell, repentance, the lake of fire, as that might offend, and cause people to leave.

The call of God on a pastor being a requirement has gone out the window for the modern-day church. In the last chapter we discussed the difference between the man-pleasing pastor and the God-called pastor. We discussed the role of the pastor and the accountability for that role in the sight of God. When a pastor accepts the role in most modern-day churches, they are offered very large salaries, with many mega benefits and all the perks of being a pastor, as long as they stay within the guidelines of what the board of directors wants them to do.

This board of directors in the modern-day church is also called an elder board. This board is supposed to be made up of men, mature in their walk with the Lord, that will help lead the church to God. I dare say that most of the elders on these boards are not in any way seeking the God of the bible because, if they were, they would be letting the pastor lead the sheep instead of the sheep leading the pastor.

These boards are not focused on God. Most of them, I dare say, are not even saved. Have you ever gone to a church and heard the pastor say they had to refer to the elder board, or the board told him to do this, or that? When you listen to Christian preaching t you will hear at times, the pastor mention that he and the board discussed this, or he and the board talked about that, or the board told him this or that. The board has become the final authority in a church in which God has established the pastor to be the final authority, and the bible to be the absolute final authority for the pastor. Any church that denies the Lord as the leader of the church, and any pastor that is leading a church that is reducing any part of the bible's authority, is a Satan worshiping church.

As I have pointed out in my first book The Office of Overseers, it does not matter if you as a pastor are under the authority of a board or not. In your role as pastor, you are accountable to God directly for that church. If that church restricts you because of the board then, Oh well, you are still held accountable to God for that church because you stepped into that God accountable position of pastor. The best thing any pastor can do is to come out from under the authority of a board that limits things for the Lord.

I spoke with a man at work about a year ago. This man was telling me how the board in his church works. This man is attending a southern Baptist church that compromises on one version of the bible being perfect and without error in the English language. The preaching, and bible topics are not to offend others. This man is a deacon for life in the church. This means he can come to deacon meetings, and make decisions for the church even though he has not stepped foot in that church for over two years. I have yet to figure that one out. This man says he knows the bible enough to make godly decisions while at the same time disobeying the bible that he says he believes. His board of directors allows the pastor to only preach for thirty-minutes. The board has decided anything longer than that is a problem as people cannot possibly expect to be in church and listen to the bible for that long. That is the excuse they use.

As I have said in every book that I have written, when you compromise your belief in one true bible, then anything goes. You will believe and do anything, you will believe that thirty minutes messages are ok, that only preaching love and joy will change people's lives. No! my dear pastor friend, it may fill the offering plate, but will not in any way change lives for Jesus Christ.

It is a sad day when pastors are longing for these kinds of churches because it is mainly for the income and the status they receive from these churches. These modern-day pastors are okay with following the guidelines set by the board because in their mind, that board is the spiritual leadership of the churches, so in their minds, they are not really accountable for what they preach. Some of these boards, I know, require the pastor to submit his outlines prior to the message to make sure it is not a negative one.

I have another friend who was in the state church in Ireland. When he was scheduled to preach, he had to submit his outline for the message a week before his scheduled preaching time, and have it approved before he could present it. I remember him calling me at times and telling me how angry he was with them because they made him remove anything that referred to salvation, as telling people that there is only one way to heaven might offend someone. If it were me, I would have just preached it once, and let the chips fall where they may. I would not be welcomed in any of these modern-day churches as I would preach the gospel which has become so offensive in many churches.

That last statement, in itself, is ironic. The church, the very word “church” implies godly origin, rejects the things of God. Pastors keep clinging to these anti-bible churches and keep compromising their beliefs. They are all being taught in the cemeteries (seminaries) they attend for four years. These schools teach them to do church the “right way” while not teaching them to follow the bible.

These new pastors coming out of cemetery are all trained with traditions of men, they have been convinced that the board knows better than the Lord, that the guidelines of the board outweigh the guidelines of the bible. Well, my dear pastor friend, I will say again if you do not believe that there is one version of the bible that is the truth, then anything goes. With the belief that the board knows best, these man-called pastors are ready to apply for that job of pastor in that church that has thousands of people coming every week.

The modern-day pastor also writes out his message. I heard it the other day from a man that was teaching people how to preach by reading books about preaching styles, and methods to motivate the congregation for results. "I'm sure that is biblical, lol," Anyway, this man was saying that he felt that the best way to preach was to use the pastor's manuscript. I thought about that for a moment, and then I realized what he was referring to. I had never heard of a pastor's manuscript. A pastor's manuscript is created by the pastor writing out every word of his message and carefully memorizing and reading it in a way that he is not staring down at the manuscript the entire time he is preaching.

In the church I grew up in, yes, an independent fundamental King James bible believing church, we had an assistant pastor that wrote out all his messages, and followed them to the letter. This is how he was taught, and trained in college. I have no issues if someone writes out a message to help them get the points of what they are trying to accomplish. However, I must ask, where is the room for the Holy Spirit to change things? Where is the room for the Holy Spirit to work? As for me, I use only an outline most of the time, although I do not really follow it. I am constantly pondering on the things of the Lord, and the message throughout the week. I have an idea of how I want the outline to go, but that is just a guide, not the manuscript of the message.

What you are reading now is the manuscript of my book. It is every word that I have written in the order in which I have written them. I truly question the call of God on a pastor's life if he has to write out every word of his message and then read it to be able to preach. The bible tells us that in the times we need to know what to say, the Lord will provide the words for us to say them. (Luke 12:12)

A man-called pastor has to be the CEO of a corporation in the modern church today, once they are “hired” by the board. This board dictates to the pastor what they can preach, what they can teach on, they restrict any working of the Holy Spirit in the church services, and most of the time they put limits on the amount of time they can preach. The board can hire and fire the pastor if they don’t like what he does. If the modern-day pastor were to preach the bible for what it says he would be escorted out of the church and removed from the property.

The pastor in the modern-day church is like the CEO of a corporation, yes that CEO can run things but only under the direction of the board of directors. I have yet to find a passage of scripture that says that God called a board of directors to shepherd his sheep. I have not found a verse in the bible that says that God will provide boards of directors to lead his churches. However, this is what we have today,

Churches today are no longer about the bible, or even the truth of the ministry. Church is all about how many people you can entice to come to church with modern music, smoke, fancy lights, satanic rock music, and many other of the worldly methods which are used at concerts to draw people in. I dare to say that many of the pastors in these modern-day churches are not even saved, and could not even lead someone to Christ if they tried. When the rapture of the church, the catching away of the saints takes place, if it were to happen on a Sunday morning, many of these modern-day churches would not even know it until they leave church that Sunday to go to lunch and see all the destruction left behind.

Yes, in these churches, people will come by the flock loads, your offerings will be in the millions, but the Holy Spirit will not be welcomed. There will be no Holy Ghost conviction on a lost person or a prodigal that needs to return to the Savior. The Spirit of God will not be welcomed. It is a sad day when the Lord is no longer invited into this church. The bible is clear that we are to seek those old paths. We are not to seek the traditions of men, but of those old paths, with hard preaching, calling out sin, with Holy Ghost conviction pouring out so the lost person or the prodigal can turn from their sin and get back to God.

2 Corinthians 2:15-17
For we are unto God a sweet savour of Christ, in them that are saved, and in them that perish: 16. To the one we are the savour of death unto death; and to the other the savour of life unto life. And who is sufficient for these things? 17. For we are not as many, which corrupt the word of God: but as of sincerity, but as of God, in the sight of God speak we in Christ. The purpose of the church is to be a light in the darkness, it is to be that place that people can go to find the Lord, and the things of the Lord. It is not to be a dance club, it is not to be a place

to make one "feel good" about themselves, it is not to be a multi-million-dollar corporation that allows anyone to just feel good about what they are buying. Church is supposed to be a place to go to meet the Lord, to have one's heart convicted of sin, and for repentance to take place. The church is to be that haven of rest and not to be a department store corporation that just gets people to shop there and then move on.

The church is a place that is supposed to speak of Jesus Christ and him crucified. The Church is not supposed to be a place that just speaks of love and giving of your money to sow your seed. The church is to be a place that stands strong on the bible being the inspired word of God without contradiction or error. The church is not a place that preaches, and teaches, all the different corruptions of the bible and say that they are "all the word of God." It is the compromising of the bible in the first place that got the modern church in the position that it is in today. The church must be about Jesus, turning people to Jesus, and getting people to live like Jesus so then God and God alone can change their lives, and their lives can be fulfilled through Jesus Christ.

The last statement of this passage is that in the sight of God we are to speak Christ, the church was originally founded on Jesus Christ, (Matthew 16:18) it is to be all about him, it is a place that God is watching. The modern church "leaders" need to realize that God is watching the error of what they are doing, and at some point, just as you, and I will, they too, will stand before a Holy God, and have to answer for what they have done. When I stand before the Lord I don't want to have to answer for leading God's church to the world, instead I want to be known for leading God's church to God.

Acts 5:27-32
And when they had brought them, they set them before the council: and the high priest asked them, 28. Saying, Did not we straitly command you that ye should not teach in this name? and, behold, ye have filled Jerusalem with your doctrine, and intend to bring this man's blood upon us. This is a great illustration of a board of directors trying to lead the first church leaders on how to do church. They told Peter and his company what they could preach on and what they could not preach on. These men had been jailed for not preaching what the so-called religious leaders wanted them to preach. The Lord removed them from the jail and now are back in front of the council.

Unlike back in this story, where Peter actually stood up to these men because they were telling him the opposite of what God was telling them as God-called pastors, Peter had convictions that were built on faith in the word of God, and the leading of the Lord. Peter's faith got stronger each, and every time he was in the word because the Holy Spirit makes the word come alive every time it is read and believed.

The modern-day pastor would have just said, "OK, I will not preach the name of Jesus Christ." These modern-day pastors wouldn't have stood up for their conviction, or their faith. Why is that? because they want to keep that large salary, that nice house, and fancy car. The modern-day pastors are living by sight and seeking what man can provide for them, and not on the faith required to run ministry God's way. The modern church board of directors were just like this “religious” council of Peter’s day. The only difference is, the modern-day pastor has stopped standing up for the things of God.

29. Then Peter and the other apostles answered and said, We ought to obey God rather than men. If the modern-day pastor would do what Peter, and the other apostles did, and tell the modern-day, God-rejecting, bible-denying churches of today that they should obey God and not man, these modern-day churches would not be as popular for pastors to run to. There would be fewer modern-day pastors compromising the bible, as many of them would realize that they are not truly called of God to pastor. With this understanding these modern-day pastors would seek the calling that God has for them. Allowing God to place them where he can use them for his glory. Instead, they go after their own glory.

30. The God of our fathers raised up Jesus, whom ye slew and hanged on a tree. 31. Him hath God exalted with his right hand to be a Prince and a Saviour, for to give repentance to Israel, and forgiveness of sins. The Lord is all about men turning from sin which allows those living in sin to turn back to God, and those that are lost to get saved. If this message is not being preached, or taught to the sheep, how will they ever make a change. How will folks ever come to a saving knowledge of Jesus Christ.

The churches of old, the churches of the bible were churches that taught the bible for what it said, their pastors sowed in tears for the people in the church. I dare bet that most of the modern-day pastors do not even pray for the people in their churches. Today, modern pastors pray for the foolishness of filling seats, and gathering offerings just like a corporate business plan. These churches hold the mindset that more people, and more money determines success.

If the modern-day church board had to oversee a small church like ours, the board would pull me into a meeting and tell me that what I am doing is not building the church. The modern church board would tell me not to be so loud when I preach, and that I need to stop telling people that they are going to hell if they reject Jesus. The word hell offends people. I would be told I need to pass an offering plate to raise more funds, and then we would have a growing church. I tell you my dear pastor friend, if you have a church of ten people or so, and all of them are seeking God with all their heart, then my friend, you have a church that is bigger in the Lord's eyes than any mega-church in the world. These mega-churches would be like Sodom just before the destruction; they would not be able to find even ten righteous people in these churches.

32. And we are his witnesses of these things; and so is also the Holy Ghost, whom God hath given to them that obey him. The apostles were witnesses, and those today that are truly seeking the things of God are witnesses also to that fact that if we do things God's way, then he will do what he has promised and bless, and strengthen us. God promises that if the things are done in these worldly churches will be gotten rid of and Holy Ghost conviction is preached through the bible, that lives can be changed, and souls can be saved.

This is what we, the saved, and those apostles back then, are witness to. It is the power of the gospel and the changing of lives that comes from the bible. No modern-day church, run as a corporation, with a board of directors, or elders, can ever have the power of the Holy Spirit on it, because they limit what God can do. Once these churches deny the working of the gospel all they have are Satan worshiping churches. These modern churches become Satan worshiping churches because the bible says that you cannot serve two masters, you will only be able to love one, and hate the other. Which type of pastor are you my dear friend, are you a pastor of a Satan-centered church or a God-centered church?

1 Timothy 6:9-21
But they that will be rich fall into temptation and a snare, and into many foolish and hurtful lusts, which drown men in destruction and perdition. 10. For the love of money is the root of all evil: which while some coveted after, they have erred from the faith, and pierced themselves through with many sorrows. The bible tells us that those that go after the money will err from the faith. That simply means that if a man-pleasing pastor seeks a pastorate at a church for what he can get out of it, he is doing it at the cost of erring from the faith.

Just because a pastor may receive a large salary does not mean that he is erring from the faith. That is not what I am saying. What I am saying is, that the man who will not do the job of the pastor unless he has certain things the church can provide, certain "compensation packages" is not truly seeking to serve God. If it is a pastor that everyone knows about and loves, he can negotiate his salary with the church as well.

For me, if a pastor has to "negotiate" his salary with a church his motives are a result of his selfish Satan serving pride, and he has no business in a church. As a God-called pastor I could not imagine ever negotiating a salary to serve the Lord, if the church offers a salary, great! If the Lord wants you to make more money he will impress it on the hearts of the people in the church to increase your salary.

I also hear pastors say that they need to go to their churches and ask for the yearly cost of living increase to their salary. These methods have come at the cost of the gospel, these pastors have erred from the faith. You may say. "Pastor, you are putting too much into it." I would say. "Oh yea, let me ask you this. What if you do ask for that "raise" because you feel you deserve it, and they say no. Are you going to quit?" If you don't quit, you will for surely begin to develop some resentment toward that church for not increasing your pay. That resentment will turn into bitterness, and soon you will be looking for another church. You will have erred from the faith for the sake of money because your initial focus was on the church as a business, and for what you could get out of it. Your error was that you did not see the church as a ministry, looking to see what the Lord could get out of it. If your ministry is focused on what the Lord could get out of it, your rewards will far exceed any raises.

11. But thou, O man of God, flee these things; and follow after righteousness, godliness, faith, love, patience, meekness. One thing about the bible is that God always has an answer for everything that we are going through in this life. Look at this verse plainly, "FLEE THESE THINGS" the bible says not to focus on the business, the money of the ministry, but we are to focus on the God of the ministry.

We are to flee the lustful desires of the money and the salary packages and to seek after righteousness, Matthew 6:33 keeps coming to mind for me. If we SEEK the things of God he will provide everything else, if we seek the things of God the salary will come, but let it come in God's time. In almost all churches today, if you had the ability to make the pastors all live by faith in their ministries, and not negotiate their salaries, there would be an influx of empty pulpits, and a reduction of business jobs available, as the man-pleasing pastors would leave the ministry, to take secular jobs and serve the money.

I am not being hateful, but I am being truthful. Are you serving as a pastor? A servant collecting heavenly treasures? Or are you a CEO collecting a paycheck? Yes, even when seeking the heavenly treasures one may have to work an outside job, one may have to be tired a lot, but keep working it, keep going, and let the God of the bible be the one you serve. If God doesn't provide for you like he said he would then he is a liar, and we all know God is not a liar.

A truly God-called pastor will seek after righteousness, faith, love, patience, meekness, and other biblical fruits. A God-called pastor will seek after the things of God, and not after the things of the world. The God-called pastor will trust God to provide for them, and not look to the world to provide for them. Oh, what a sad day it will be when those man-pleasing pastors have to stand before the God of the bible, and have to answer for serving the god of this world, which is Satan, by seeking the money instead of seeking the kingdom of God.

12. Fight the good fight of faith, lay hold on eternal life, whereunto thou art also called, and hast professed a good profession before many witnesses. Timothy was a man that was called to do service for the Lord in the area of preaching as an evangelist. Timothy was helping the churches to move forward for the things of the Lord, encouraging them to be in their bibles, or what they had of the bible at that time. He encouraged them to obey sound doctrines. Paul is telling Timothy here, to fight the good fight, seek eternal life, he is called unto eternal life because he is saved, he is also called to ministry by the Lord. Timothy has professed a good testimony before many witnesses, he is truly seeking the God of the bible, and the God of the bible has met all of his needs along the way. We must make our focus the Lord, and not the money. We cannot serve two masters, because we will love one and hate the other.

13. I give thee charge in the sight of God, who quickeneth all things, and before Christ Jesus, who before Pontius Pilate witnessed a good confession; 14. That thou keep this commandment without spot, unrebukeable, until the appearing of our Lord Jesus Christ: Paul is telling Timothy that he is to keep seeking the work of the ministry, and not to make a bad name for that ministry, or the Lord, that he is to seek the things of God in a humble manner. The God-called man must not seek the money, which at some point will make him angry or jealous. The money will make the man think that he is something when in reality, he is nothing. Timothy, as with truly God-called pastors, seek the ministry of the Lord without blame, without any spots in that ministry. We are to walk circumspectly in the things of God looking and watching every step that is made, so our steps and actions will honor the Lord.

15. Which in his times he shall shew, who is the blessed and only Potentate, the King of kings, and Lord of lords; 16. Who only hath immortality, dwelling in the light which no man can approach unto; whom no man hath seen, nor can see: to whom be honour and power everlasting. Amen. 17. Charge them that are rich in this world, that they be not highminded, nor trust in uncertain riches, but in the living God, who giveth us richly all things to enjoy; The bible tells us not that money is bad, a large salary package is not bad, there is no sin in receiving these kinds of gifts. The bible says that all these are for our enjoyment, but the bible is telling the rich that they are not to be high minded, they are not to be selfish, and only seeking the money of the world.

This is the problem with money, if one has money, and is not in the bible, and are not seeking God diligently, then they will begin to focus on that money, and not on the Lord, or the ministry. The person seeking money will slowly begin to serve that money, and not the Lord. Blessed is the one that has a lot of money, and is still focused on the Lord, blessed is the man that has the money, and knows that that is the Lord's money and he is to honor God with that money. Blessed is that man that has the money but serves the Lord.

18. That they do good, that they be rich in good works, ready to distribute, willing to communicate; 19. Laying up in store for themselves a good foundation against the time to come, that they may lay hold on eternal life. Those that have money in the ministry, and are receiving the large salary packages, and still serve the Lord, and not the money; are to lay up some of the money for the difficult times and have some excess for giving to the ministry. The bible here says they are to be ready to distribute, willing to communicate, they are to be willing to give to the Lord, and the things of the ministry.

Not one person ever in this world, has been able to outgive God. It is a good thing if God has blessed you financially to distribute some of that excess to the things, and needs of God's ministry, or the needs of the people in God's ministry. If you give to the needs of the ministry, the Lord will always repay with extra those of a pure heart that gave to him.

20. O Timothy, keep that which is committed to thy trust, avoiding profane and vain babblings, and oppositions of science falsely so called: 21. Which some professing have erred concerning the faith. Grace be with thee. Amen. The warning to Timothy here was that he was to keep that which was committed to his trust. That which was committed to his trust was his calling into the ministry. Timothy was not called to serve a large salary package, that is what the man-pleasing pastors do, they are serving the god of this world, which is Satan.

Timothy was to keep that calling that God had placed on his life, he was to avoid the desires of the flesh, the desires for riches, the whispers of Satan being placed in the ears of people. The bible says that those that seek after other things beside that which was committed to their trust have erred from the faith, they have neglected the bible and the gospel, and have focused on the sinful desires of the world.

Erred simply defined is: *to violate an accepted standard of conduct; to stray.* The latter being the meaning here, those that are not called of God, and are not seeking that calling, will err from the faith. The man-pleasing pastor also will err from the faith as they will violate the standards that God has put in place and go after the money, and not the Lord.

Romans 8:5-8
For they that are after the flesh do mind the things of the flesh; but they that are after the Spirit the things of the Spirit. 6. For to be carnally minded is death; but to be spiritually minded is life and peace. 7. Because the carnal mind is enmity against God: for it is not subject to the law of God, neither indeed can be. 8. So then they that are in the flesh cannot please God. A man that is seeking the things of the world is, in essence, seeking Satan and his devices. If he is a saved man, that is on the outside serving God but is focused on the rewards of man, and not the treasures of God, his mind is in a carnal state, he is at enmity with God, working against God, and he can never please God as long as he is in that state of mind. The carnal man, the saved person with his focus on the things of the world will ALWAYS be against the things of God. It is not that they reject the things of God but, they work in rebellion toward the things of God.

A carnal man will rebel against the things of God, where a natural man will reject the things of God, there is a difference between rebelling and rejecting. The man that rebels against the things of God knows what he is supposed to do, he knows what is right and he is refusing to do what he is called to do. Remember Jonah? The lost man does not see or know the truth of the Lord until he comes to salvation, he is rejecting it because he does not see it as truth. The man that knows the truth and rebels against it is more accountable than the man that does not know the truth. (James 4:17)

Matthew 6:24

No man can serve two masters: for either he will hate the one, and love the other; or else he will hold to the one, and despise the other. Ye cannot serve God and mammon. The bible is clear here that you cannot serve both God and money, you must pick one. The man-pleasing pastor has made his choice to serve the money. The fruits of his ministry will be taking people away from the faith of the Lord, it will be taking people away from the truth of the bible, it will be a Satan serving ministry, and not a God-centered ministry.

The God-called pastor has made his choice, he has chosen to serve God, he has chosen to lead people to God, he has chosen to lead people to their bibles, he has chosen to teach people how to seek the God of the bible, he has chosen that even if he has to sacrifice everything he has for the Lord, he has chosen to do so. The work of the Lord can move forward, because he knows by faith that God will meet every need along the way.

The God-called pastor will be focused on God, and how God wants things done no matter what he may receive from the Lord. The God-called pastor will do the work he is called to do even if he does it for free, because he is not working for himself, but is working for the Lord. My dear pastor friend, make your choice, either serve the money of the ministry and be a CEO of a business, or choose the God of the ministry and be a servant of the Lord. Great is the reward of those that serve the Lord.

PASTORS OF OLD

Jeremiah 6:16
Thus saith the LORD, Stand ye in the ways, and see, and ask for the old paths, where is the good way, and walk therein, and ye shall find rest for your souls. But they said, We will not walk therein.

There is something to be said of the pastors of old, the ones that God directly spoke to, the ones that were willing to give their lives for their calling from the Lord. I ask myself sometimes. What made these pastors so much different than the pastors of today? The pastors of today are weak, and selfish, focused on what they can get from the ministry. How much money can they make, how big a church can they build but, the pastors of old were sacrificial, and strong. The difference is, they actually believed in the God they were serving, they actually believed in following the calling that God had placed on their lives, and they were not afraid to follow that calling. They did not question that calling, they just obeyed that calling, and believed that God would do what he said he would do.

Here in the United States, and I imagine, in other countries as well, the commercialization of the church, and the pastorate has removed the holiness from the ministry, and has allowed sin to rule and reign in the local churches today. The Pastors are cowards, they will not stand up for the truth of the bible because they will be removed from their pulpits, they will lose their large salaries, they will not be able to live in their large houses. These pastors are weak in their faith at best, because they are not in their bibles, so they quit at every difficult situation that comes about.

Most of these pastors fight the battles between ministry, family, and a job but they refuse to fight this battle God's way, and they always end up losing. The pastors of today wants everyone to be their friend. They want everyone to like them, they speak only nice things to their congregations so they do not offend the board of elders, and the people in the church.

The church board has become a human resources department for the church, they are monitoring everything preached and taught. These boards don't care if the truth is taught because if the truth is taught people will get offended, and leave. All they want are soft spoken momma boys that have no back bones to stand up for the things of the Lord.

Look at the small truly bible believing churches of today. Although very small in numbers, most of them cannot even pay their pastors, they go out and visit, and knock-on doors. These small churches do all this, and all that, and have very little results. Why? These churches preach the truth, and many people reject that truth. Only a very few come, but the truth is being preached.

The pastors of old did not care about your money, or anyone else's feelings, they preached the truth. They did not care if you, I, or the man down the street showed up for church or not. These old time pastors did not care if they had thousands listening to them or not, they preached the truth of the bible, they preached it hard, and they preached it long, they let God sort it all out. In the church of today we no longer let God do anything in the church, he is not allowed to lead the service, he is not allowed to convict hearts from sinful ways, he is not even allowed to draw people to himself, the pastors of today have been part of the removal of the Lord from the local churches.

The pastors of old would not stand for the pastors of today. The pastors of old would treat the pastors of today like Pharisees calling them a generation of vipers, pansies, and momma boys that go and suck their thumbs, because someone in the church did not like them. The pastors of old would kick out the pastors of today from God's churches, for their cowardice.

In the ministry, as a pastor, people will not like you. People will sometimes hate you, call you names, and then try to blame it on the bible because they know better, yet they are not in the bible or seeking God for themselves. If we want the "God results" in our churches today, that the pastors of old had, we must follow the examples that they set.

I have determined, as a pastor, that I want bible level Christianity, I want that kind of Christianity that men like Elijah, Paul, Jeremiah, Enoch, and many others in the bible had. These men of God obeyed the calling that God put on their lives, they suffered hardships for the Lord, and they reaped the blessings from the Lord as a result. The pastors of old saw people come to God, they saw people's changed lives for the Lord. When they died, they saw the fruits of their labors fulfilled in heaven, and the many souls that were there as a result of doing what they were supposed to do.

The pastors of today will not see their fruits in heaven, they are not laying up treasures for themselves in heaven, they are reaping the man-made treasures of today not caring for the souls of tomorrow. They are not focused on the truth of the bible but only on the false truth of themselves. Many pastors of today are not even saved, and almost all of them reject the truth of the bible. Today's pastor will say. "Look at how I built this church." The pastors of old would weep and thank God for him building his church, his way.

There is a movement in today's churches that says "We must change the way we are doing church. We must adjust it for society of today. We must make church more appealing to the younger generation so they will come to church." I hear pastors all the time say. "The old ways are ancient, they do not work, people are not like they used to be back then." Well my dear pastor friend, if you read and study your bible, then show me where in the Old Testament to the New Testament, did the message of the cross change? Where did the methods of preaching change? Where did they forsake the old ways and go to the new ways? You will never find that in the bible because it is not there. God is the same yesterday, today, and forever and he changes not, the bible says, so if the God of the bible does not change, then why must we change the ways of God in the ministry?

The pastors of today look at churches like ours, King James Bible preaching, teaching, church that loves people, that is seeking to direct them to God, they look at our very small country churches, that are clinging to the old hymns, that bring only bibles to church, the old altar calling churches, the no smoke, and rock band churches, and they say, " Oh, those churches are small because they are doing things like our grandfathers used to do them. The modern-day pastors convince themselves that because the churches like ours are small, and mostly older people, that these churches are dying and if they want to build the church for the future they need to change everything they are doing so they can fill the seats.

Today's pastor is only focused on building his church for today, he has no interest in God's church for the future. The modern pastors are not laying up treasures in heaven, but are laying them up here on earth and enjoying the fruits of their labours here and now, while missing that eternal reward altogether. I am just an ignorant pastor when it comes to building churches, and ministry. I am learning as I go but, one thing I can say is that, I believe the bible with all my heart, mind, and soul, and as long as I focus on laying up heavenly treasure for the Lord he will reward me with earthly treasures, and he will fill his churches along the way. I must remain on that old path. Hey, after all, that old path is not being traveled a lot anymore so the path should not be too crowded.

I will say, for me and the church God has placed me in, we will take a pass from the new ways, and just cling to the Old paths. Why? Because the bible says for us to do so. This is God's church not mine. God is responsible for putting butts in the seats, for convicting hearts, minds, and lives to get changed, it is God that does that, not me. I'll just preach my heart out and let him sort it all out.

Making the church today conform to the world is NOT a biblical way to build a church. Using worldly methods is a rejection of the bible, and the truth of the bible, to change the church today. The bible CLEARLY tells us that we are to SEEK the old paths, seek the old ways of doing church, and the ministry. Do not look at the example of you fathers for how to have full churches, but to your grandfathers, your great grandfathers, the men in the bible they all had the one thing in common, they all followed the old paths and they got bible level Christianity, not this lazy, Satan-serving Christianity we see today.

Like always, let's go to the bible and see some men in the bible that got to that bible level Christianity, because they sought those old paths and preached the truth and let God do what only he can do. We will first start with one of my heroes of the bible, the prophet Elijah.

Elijah was a very rough man, he said things as they were, he did not sugar coat anything, and he had a relationship with God like only very few have ever had. Elijah was a man that had truly sought FIRST the kingdom of God, and all of its righteousness, knowing that everything else was going to be added unto him. We will go to the events on Mount Carmel, where there was a showdown between the four-hundred and fifty prophets of (Baal), Satan, and one prophet of God.

For the man of God to be successful, and to have the kind of relationship, and power from God that Elijah had, he must have been walking with God, he must have had the sin removed from his life. Elijah was a prophet that sought the old paths, he was not a quitter as many are today. Elijah was a man that stood the test, he held the course, and saw the victory. Oh, how much more the gospel would increase if the man of God would actually be the man of God, and not just a hireling, not just someone that quits at every turn.

As I said before, I am on some of the social media sites and pages called “pastors seeking churches.” There are an alarming number of so-called pastors on these sites that say that they have twenty years of pastoral experiences in several different churches, and they are looking to serve as interim, and pulpit supply. I look at that kind of post, and man, red flags come to mind. First of all, having several different churches on one's resume is not a good thing in the ministry, it shows that that pastor is not willing to stand the course. Second, the fact that you have that experience, and are still looking for a church, makes me wonder why you have not stayed at one church, and why you are no longer in the ministry?

The pastor on this search site will say they want to serve God as an interim pastor or pulpit supply. They are saying that they are not interested in making a long-term commitment, they are not interested in holding the course and they only want to do it when it is convenient for them to do so. Most of these same pastors will ask to stay in a certain area. I saw a man the other day that said it did not matter what denomination he would pulpit supply wherever the Lord wanted.

I will tell you my friend, the Lord is not going to put you in a church, even to fill the pulpit, of a denomination that is not seeking him, the pulpit of a church that denies the truth of the bible, of a denomination that accepts sin, so you can present "yourself" to them. This is the shape that the ministry in the United States has gotten into. Sin has overtaken the churches here, and this is why we need to be reminded of keeping our dedication to the Lord, and to doctrines of the church that the men of God in the bible displayed. We must follow their examples. If we want God to move we must cleave to the calling to which he has called us. If not, and we are NOT called, we need to leave the ministry because all we are doing is hurting the ministry at that point.

1 Kings 18:17-40
And it came to pass, when Ahab saw Elijah, that Ahab said unto him, Art thou he that troubleth Israel? 18. And he answered, I have not troubled Israel; but thou, and thy father's house, in that ye have forsaken the commandments of the Lord, and thou hast followed Baalim. Elijah is telling the king here that it is not him (Elijah) preaching the truth, that has gotten Israel all in an uproar but it is the fact that the king, and the people have clung to the things of Satan, and they are worshiping a god of Satan (Baal), and not the God of the bible.

Notice that Elijah says that they have FORSAKEN the commandments of the Lord, they have left the things of God and they have followed the ways of Satan. I will tell you my dear pastor friend, and this may upset you, but that man that is just filling in, that has been to many different churches as pastor, and leaves every time the going gets tough, or for a larger salary or benefits, is no better than the prophets of Baalim, he is leading the people away from the Lord.

If he is not dedicated to the things of the Lord but only to the things of himself, how can he ever expect to lead people to the things of God. It is simple, you are either on the Lord's side or you are on Satan's side, there is no middle ground, it is impossible to serve two masters. Elijah was putting the responsibility back on Ahab, and Ahab's prophets that were only hirelings. It was those that served Baalim that were the problem, not Elijah, who shares the truth. If, and when, I go on these sites, I may comment once in a while about quitting, and not staying the course. I may ask a question in a way that puts the truth up front, and I will be hated for that.

19 Now therefore send, and gather to me all Israel unto mount Carmel, and the prophets of Baal four hundred and fifty, and the prophets of the groves four hundred, which eat at Jezebel's table. Elijah has had enough of Ahab and his rebellion against the things of God. Elijah knows he has the power of God on him at this moment, and he says to Ahab. Go get all your prophets, which are four-hundred and fifty, and then go and get all of your wife's prophets also, which is another four hundred and bring them to me..

Elijah is saying here, I have had enough of this blatant rebellion. Once and for all we are going to show you who the real God is. We are going to show you the power of the God of heaven and earth, and we are going to show you who is the one that is troubling Israel. For Elijah to be able to do this, he cannot be just a hireling, as an hireling does not have the power of God on them. A hireling has only the power of self and pride on them.

When a man gets the power of God on his life, he is a force that cannot be stopped by man. Elijah was a true man of God. He placed his life in jeopardy here. Nearly every soul in the nation hated him, and now, it is he alone with God, versus the eight hundred and fifty servants of Satan. Remember Elijah sought the OLD paths.

20. So Ahab sent unto all the children of Israel, and gathered the prophets together unto mount Carmel. 21. And Elijah came unto all the people, and said, How long halt ye between two opinions? if the Lord be God, follow him: but if Baal, then follow him. And the people answered him not a word. Elijah is telling the people that are watching that they need to get off that fence, they need to either pick one side or the other just as Joshua told the people this, the Lord told the people this, it is either one side or the other, no more middle ground.

For you pastors out there pick your side, and pick it now, either go to God's side and actually be a pastor after God's own heart or go to Satan's side and be a hireling. You cannot do both because you will hurt yourself and others.

Imagine the scene here. It is Elijah by himself, and the eight hundred plus prophets, the king, and his wife, and many spectators. What a scene it must have been to see the power of God come down from heaven to set things straight. The man of God must be called of God to do the things of God, plain and simple, anything else is serving Satan.

22. Then said Elijah unto the people, I, even I only, remain a prophet of the Lord; but Baal's prophets

are four hundred and fifty men. Elijah has identified that he is all alone, he is on the mountain with the prophets of Baal. The other prophets were of Jezebel and they were there watching but, it was the prophets of Baal on the mountain top with Elijah. Baal was a god that was made by man for man to worship, Baal was an image that was worshiped by the people. The people who worshiped this image were worshiping Satan as well.

23. Let them therefore give us two bullocks; and let them choose one bullock for themselves, and cut it in pieces, and lay it on wood, and put no fire under: and I will dress the other bullock, and lay it on wood, and put no fire under: 24. And call ye on the name of your gods, and I will call on the name of the Lord: and the God that answereth by fire, let him be God. And all the people answered and said, It is well spoken. Elijah sets the scene here and tells the prophets to get two bullocks. Bullock simply defined is: *a young bull; a castrated bull.*

Elijah says get two young bulls, you take one and kill it, cut it up, lay it on the altar. We will NOT start a fire under it. You prophets of Baal, call on your gods. I will do the same thing with my young bullock, and I will call on the God of heaven. The one that brings the fire down from heaven and lights the sacrifice on the altar, is the God that we will all serve. The people said, that is smart, let's do that. So they prepared to do this showdown between Baal and God to see who was more powerful.

We know through salvation and faith in the bible that God is always more powerful. However, Elijah offers this challenge. The bible does not say that God told him to issue this challenge, it does not say that God said. “I will make sure you get what you need.” Elijah had a close relationship with God, Elijah was called by God to do the work of God, and by him surrendering to the will of God for his life he gets to see the power of God work by his hand. It is ONLY a person walking with God that gets this kind of bible level Christianity that can do what Elijah is about to do, today.

The pastors of today do not do what the pastors of old did because they are not walking with God as they did back then. Where in the bible does it say that that kind of fire- praying power has left the people of God? We hear of it again in many places in the bible, and in the book of Acts chapter two, when the holy Ghost showed up at the house at Pentecost that great power was seen. Yet, we do not see this power anymore today because we are not walking with God like these men did.

I have been on a personal journey, for the past five years, to get to that bible level Christianity. I cannot at this time, pray down fire from heaven, but we can, and do see the Holy Spirit move at times. We see the impossible starting to become possible, we see the unexpected becoming reality, we see the lost coming to Jesus and the wandering coming back to the fold. That, my dear pastor friend, is what happens when the man of God, the truly God-called man does things God’s way and is not just a hireling that is in it for himself.

25. And Elijah said unto the prophets of Baal, Choose you one bullock for yourselves, and dress it first; for ye are many; and call on the name of your gods, but put no fire under. 26. And they took the bullock which was given them, and they

dressed it, and called on the name of Baal from morning even until noon, saying, O Baal, hear us. But there was no voice, nor any that answered. And they leaped upon the altar which was made. The challenge has begun, the prophets of Baal, the hirelings, they have placed their sacrifice on the altar, they have placed all the decorations all around it, they are now calling on their false idol, they are calling on one of the gods of Satan to bring down the fire from heaven, and to prove who is the true God.

May will say with this book that I am attacking pastors which I am in no way doing. But, folks, let's be real for a moment. We do not have much time left before the return of the Lord, and we need to stop displaying a false god that will lead people to hell. The bible calls out this sin, the Lord calls out this sin throughout the bible, and if God is against it we should be too.

Many have chosen today to not speak up against this sin, and the sin in the churches because it is not popular to do so, and we are paying a heavy price for that now. We see churches full of people that are as lost and on their way to hell. When they leave the church service they are in the same condition spiritually as they were when they arrived. We see people having religious experiences but no conviction from the Holy Spirit. We see pastors who are cowards, compromising the truth because they want to keep their jobs, which they never should have sought after to begin with. If you are a pastor, and you think of your pastorate as a job, then my friend, you need to get out because you are not in it for the Lord, or you have lost your vision.

These prophets of Baal were calling on their god all morning, the bible says until noon. They spent hours calling on their god. I'm sure they were dancing, pleading, cutting themselves, and whatever else they do when people worship Satan. The false prophets heard NO voice from their god, they heard no answer from their god. This made them even more determined. They felt that they needed to jump on the altar, maybe in an effort to get the attention of their god and yet, all morning, no god answered.

When a pastor is just a hireling, refuses to seek the God of the bible, and would rather do things for their own gain they are just as lost and dead as these prophets of Baal. These false prophets have not one single connection with God. Their prayers, even as pastors, do not get heard because they have sins blocking the ear of God. We must get back to the bible to get the power of God back in our churches and allow ONLY God-called men to pastor these churches, not just put someone in place for no reason. If a person is in the pastorate, and they are not called of God the best that church will ever see is Baal worship, if it is not of God it is of Satan.

27. And it came to pass at noon, that Elijah mocked them, and said, Cry aloud: for he is a god; either he is talking, or he is pursuing, or he is in a journey, or peradventure he sleepeth, and must be awaked. 28. And they cried aloud, and cut themselves after their manner with knives and lancets, till the blood gushed out upon them. 29. And it came to pass, when midday was past, and they prophesied until the time of the offering of the evening sacrifice, that there was neither voice, nor any to answer, nor any that regarded. I like this part though. I'm not sure I would mock the false prophets in a showdown. But, if you have that mountain moving faith of the bible, you can with confidence do this. Even now, I am not mocking or making fun, I am just calling out their behavior according to the bible.

Elijah was mocking these prophets. He was saying, in a sense. "Hey guys! you've been here all day, you've cried, and danced. Is your god busy talking to someone, that he is not paying attention to you? Is he maybe chasing someone, and forgot about you? Maybe he is just asleep, and needs to be awakened?" This made the prophets angry with Elijah because they had done all these activities and had no answer from their god.

It is like the churches of today. You may have the large numbers in your seats, but where are the lives that are changing for the Lord, where are the souls getting saved, where are the people surrendering to the ministry, where are the things of God being seen through the people? They are not being seen because these churches and their leaders are not seeking or worshiping God. These churches are no different than the people here that are serving Satan, the false god.

Pastor, let me ask you some questions. Why is there no power of God in your church? Why are souls just as lost when they leave your church as they were when they arrived? Why are the lives of people in your church still the same and spiritually, they are in the same condition year after year? Because many are not searching for the God of the bible but the god of this world, which is Satan. Sin has run rampant in this nation and much of it has been allowed to come in from the pulpit. May God have mercy on our souls. What will your answer be when you face the God of the bible at your judgment, and he asks, how come you led your church to serve Satan and not the God of the bible?

30. And Elijah said unto all the people, Come near unto me. And all the people came near unto him. And he repaired the altar of the Lord that was broken down. Elijah said ok I've had enough, you've had enough time. It is now high time to get out of the way, and let me do what I need to do so we can see that my God, who is the God of gods, he that is the ruler of all work. He took that altar that the false prophets broke and repaired it. All the people are gathered around, and now the show begins.

31. And Elijah took twelve stones, according to the number of the tribes of the sons of Jacob, unto whom the word of the Lord came, saying, Israel shall be thy name: 32. And with the stones he built an altar in the name of the Lord: and he made a trench about the altar, as great as would contain two measures of seed. 33. And he put the wood in order, and cut the bullock in pieces, and laid him on the wood, and said, Fill four barrels with water, and pour it on the burnt sacrifice, and on the wood. 34. And he said, Do it the second time. And they did it the second time. And he said, Do it the third time. And they did it the third time. 35. And the water ran round about the altar; and he filled the trench also with water. Elijah took the twelve stones, which represented the twelve tribes of Israel, showing that he is wrapping that altar in the presence of God's people, and he is making that altar acceptable.

Elijah had a close relationship with God. He knew that he was walking with the Lord, he knew that he had God on his side, even if God had not shown up right then, he still would have known that God was God. God did not need this display on Carmel to show that he is God. This demonstration of God's power shows that the man of God, the truly God-called man, had the power of God on his life.

Elijah was not a lukewarm pastor, he was not a commercialized pastor, he was a man that walked with God, and God used him to get things done for his glory. When Elijah had that altar soaked in water, each time it was approximately 3.5 gallons, and then he added two more times to that. Elijah had approximately ten and a half gallons of water that soaked the altar. Elijah needed to show just how powerful his God is. Elijah's God is the same God we serve. Elijah soaked the altar in water to show just how powerful God is by making that altar absolutely impossible for man to light because of how wet it was. For with God, nothing is impossible. When you have a truly God-called pastor things will get done for the Lord, souls will get saved, and lives will change, all will draw closer to God for he is who he is.

When the man-pleasing pastor gets to his church, he is only looking at the church as his next church instead of his permanent church. He has no interest in the things of God, he has no interest in doing things God's way. All he is after is the next best opportunity, or the next biggest church. I see this all the time. So-called pastors are saying how much experience they have in churches. But they have gotten the experience by running from church to church, leaving just in time for the trouble to start, and not growing in grace through these trials.

The man-pleasing pastor will always be looking for the large crowd because that is how he judges success. He will be looking for the large offerings, and the amount of people on staff, instead of being willing to work a job if needed. Keep in mind, the apostles worked jobs while doing ministry as well. Sadly, these man-pleasing pastors will always leave, and are always looking to leave the ministry at some point.

The pastorate is not a career opportunity for a person, it is not a corporate job for benefits, and salaries. The pastors of old took their calling from God as their life service to the Lord doing it in any situation, enduring whatever hardship, and living by faith in the Lord. And you know what? The pastors of old had the power of God on them, the newer pastors have the approval of man on them.

36. And it came to pass at the time of the offering of the evening sacrifice, that Elijah the prophet came near, and said, Lord God of Abraham, Isaac, and of Israel, let it be known this day that thou art God in Israel, and that I am thy servant, and that I have done all these things at thy word. 37. Hear me, O Lord, hear me, that this people may know that thou art the Lord God, and that thou hast turned their heart back again. 38. Then the fire of the Lord fell, and consumed the burnt sacrifice, and the wood, and the stones, and the dust, and licked up the water that was in the trench. The prayer was ready to be made. Elijah, the man of God, had his walk with God focused on God. Elijah prayed to God, and God heard his prayer. Not only did God hear his prayer but, God answered his prayer by bringing down that fire upon the altar.

That fire God sent down also consumed all that was there; it consumed the bullock, the wood, the stones, the dust, and licked up the water that was in the trench around the altar. Imagine if you will, for a moment having that kind of praying power on your life, and in your church, as a God-called pastor. Imagine, if you will, being able to pray for something, and it comes true. God-called pastors that are seeking God, will have what a man-pleasing pastor never could, that is the power of God on their lives and in their ministry.

When a God-called man clings to his calling from the Lord, he is surrendered to the whole calling, not just the parts he likes. The God Called pastor is committed to enduring the hardships, not just leaving when they come, he is resolved to stay the course knowing beyond a doubt that the power of the almighty God from on high is fully backing all that he is doing. And man, what a power that is! The power of God through the word of God is what saves souls, it is what changes lives, it is what draws people closer to God.

Just as the bible tells us in I Corinthians 2:14, that the natural man, the lost man, cannot receive the things of God because those things are spiritually discerned, in other words, for the lost to receive the things of God he must be saved. The same principle applies to the man pleasing pastor. If the man pleasing pastor is in his pastorate. These men are there against what God wants. These men may have the knowledge of their "job" but they will never, nor can they ever get that power of God on their ministry, as they are not receiving the things of God because they are in it for themselves and not for the Lord.

It would be better today for all the man-pleasing pastors to resign their pulpits and let the pulpits sit empty for a while than to continue in this nonsense of lukewarm pastors who are at best, developing weak, lukewarm, baby Christians. Oh, how for some, the judgment is gonna be a difficult place for them. We need more men in the pulpits like Elijah who sought God no matter the cost, who clung to their calling.

39. And when all the people saw it, they fell on their faces: and they said, The Lord, he is the God; the Lord, he is the God. 40. And Elijah said unto them, Take the prophets of Baal; let not one of them escape. And they took them: and Elijah brought them down to the brook Kishon, and slew them there. Once the power of God showed up the man of God got rid of the evil that was there. As pastors we must also rebuke the evil that continually tries to infiltrate our churches.

Man-pleasing pastors will never speak out against sin in their churches because it will drive people away from the church, it will reduce the numbers, it will reduce the salary. But oh, they forget that at the end, in eternity, they are not held accountable to the people but they are held accountable to God, and they will stand before God and give an answer one day. See, even if a man-pleasing pastor is put in place as a pastor he is still held accountable TO GOD for that pastorate (Jeremiah 23:1-2). People in LGBTQWERT, movement that are filling pulpits, yes, they will answer to God for their lifestyle sins, but they are doubly accountable to God for leading his sheep astray, and God will judge them for that pastorate, and the mockery they made of it.

A man-pleasing pastor makes a mockery of the pastorate as they will never preach the truth of the bible, if all you are seeking is the approval of man, you will never preach the truth of the bible because the truth of the bible is rejected by most people, even saved people reject some of the truths of the bible. We saw in this passage that when the people saw the God-called man, call down the power of God on his altar, and that power showed up, they turned to God, they did not turn to the man, they did not turn to Elijah, they turned to God himself.

When the power of God showed up on the men of God, the pastors of old, people came to God, they gave their lives, all they had, and all they ever were to God. These people were blessed more by giving themselves to the Lord than by any earthly thing that could be done for them. To God be the glory, thank you Elijah for the example you set for the men of today. The man-pleasing pastor will never put in the work of self-growth through the bible to draw closer to God, he will focus on programs.

We will look at one more prophet, a God-called man, and the situation he was facing, and that is the prophet Jeremiah. Jeremiah is known as the weeping prophet, he was a man that had a broken heart for his people, he had a broken heart because the people rejected the things of God, they rejected those old paths, and the judgment for their sin was coming upon them.

Today's churches have sin visiting upon them because they have forsaken those old paths. The man-pleasing pastors of today who seek to leave a ministry, or are looking for the next church, and are all about the programs, other men's works, other men's programs. These man-pleasing pastors seek out other men's outlines so they can preach them for themselves, instead of teaching the people how to look for God.

The bible is clear that we, as pastors, are to seek the Lord through his word, to lead our people to the OLD paths, and not this mumbo-jumbo new program-oriented man pleasing style of “worship” that we see today. When a pastor allows for the things of the world to be incorporated in the worship of almighty God, we have a pastor leading his people away from God, and not to God.

We will see in the next passages what those old paths are like, and how, if God-called pastors would truly cling to these old paths, then the people will cling to the old paths as well. If the man-pleasing pastor would cling to the old paths he would see that he needs to resign, and find the calling that God has put on his life, so he can reach souls for the Lord.

Oh how the pastorate has changed to please man, but not to seek God. Oh, the destruction that waits for the man-pleasing pastor for leading the people away from the God of the bible. Oh, how the power of the almighty has forsaken many of the churches because they have kicked God out by bringing in men pleasers.

Jeremiah 6:16-19
Thus saith the Lord, Stand ye in the ways, and see, and ask for the old paths, where is the good way, and walk therein, and ye shall find rest for your souls. But they said, We will not walk therein. For all the pastors that may be reading this, we must understand that the path to the old ways is not a preference, it is not negotiable, it is not a “well that’s how my parents did it” kind of a thing. Seeking

the Old Paths is a direct command from God himself, and yet we today have no interest in seeking these old paths.

I had to ask myself. Why do many people in man-led churches today not like the old paths? And, why do the independent Baptist churches all cling to their old hymns and old styles? After seeking God on this for a time, and dabbling in some of the more modern ways, the Holy Spirit through this verse, and study of the word of God, convicted my heart to see that seeking the Old paths is a command from God. God has promised that if we, as pastors, follow those old paths, God will do what he says he will do.

If we as pastors preach like the men in the bible preached, if we rebuke sin like the men in the bible did, if we edify the body of Christ like the men in the bible did, then we will end up with the same results. New age ideas, programs, and modern worship are all from rebellion against the bible and the things of God. How can a person argue with this verse?

The bible says that we are to stand in the ways and see. We are to look out among our current conditions of life, we are to find the old path, and then we are to seek that old path. The man-pleasing (man-called) pastor will never seek the old paths because he is not standing in the ways and looking for that old path. The Lord has proven it here, in our little church in New York, that while we are on these old paths he is bringing people in, he is changing lives, and saving souls. The people are staying the course, they are serving in the church, and they are themselves seeking the God of the bible. The Old paths are the way to God, they are commanded by God to be sought, but yet they are so rejected, just as the end of this verse says.

The Lord tells us that in those old paths, we will find that peace for our souls. Because, in the old paths, we learn to walk with God, we learn to talk with God, we learn to let God be God, and he rewards exceptionally as a result of it. On those old paths we learn to weather the storm, we learn to hold the course, we endure the hardships, and we rejoice in the victories like never before. But as in this verse the people say we WILL NOT walk therein.

The people chose to live in the ways that please man, and man-pleasing pastors are leading them down those new paths, and destruction is sure to come. The pastors of old knew better, they had a fear of God, along with that fear of God, they had a love for him and it increased their faith, and made them strong in the ways of the Lord. The man-pleasing pastor is placed in these modern churches that refuse to seek those old paths by the people that reject the old paths, so they all feel good about themselves only to end up burning in a lake of fire for all eternity.

17. Also I set watchmen over you, saying, Hearken to the sound of the trumpet. But they said, We will not hearken. The Lord is still talking here as he is telling the people, listen, not only am I telling you to seek the old paths, God says I,(meaning himself) has set a watchman over the people. That watchman is the God-called pastor. Anytime God is telling the people that there is a man of God over them to lead them, the bible always says that it is God that put that person there, not man.

The Lord clearly says that he has placed a God-called watchman over the people to warn them, as pastors of today should be doing by telling the people to listen to the trumpet, listen to the alarm sounding because the danger is coming, but the people refused to do so. When the people choose NOT to listen, they are no longer interested in the things or the ways of God, all they are interested in are the things that make their sin feel good, and allow them in their minds to live a conviction free life that will never honor the God of the bible.

Then these people that get mad and reject the warnings of the God-called man leave the church, and form their own "churches." Those that reject the Bible appoint man-pleasing pastors, which is what we have today. The reason we have thousands of different denominations, and beliefs is because people have refused the warning from the man of God. The man-pleasing pastor will never sound the warning because the people will not like him, so he allows them all to go straight to hell without sounding the warning. Oh! the blood that will be on these men's hands.

The God-called pastor has a battle on his hands. To sound the warning he must preach, and teach against the sins of the people in his congregation, he must make people uncomfortable, he must direct them to God, and the people sometimes hate him for doing so. Let me remind you my dear pastor friend, as a God-called pastor you have ALL the power of the almighty God backing you up, you don't need man's approval for a God-ordained position that he has placed you in. Woe be to the pastors that scatter the sheep. (Jeremiah 23:1)

18. Therefore hear, ye nations, and know, O congregation, what is among them. 19. Hear, O earth: behold, I will bring evil upon this people, even the fruit of their thoughts, because they have not hearkened unto my words, nor to my law, but rejected it. The Lord is still talking here, he is telling the people that since they refused to heed to the warnings of the trumpet, that evil will come upon the people. Many will say I am being ridiculous to say that the modern churches of today are having evil visited upon them. Well, all I can say is, when we allow men with sinful lifestyles to stand behind the pulpits and lead the so-called people of God, that is sin.

When we no longer preach messages that make people uncomfortable, when people are not getting right with God because the word is not being preached, when the church is more focused on programs than preaching, then we have allowed sin to enter. When the man-pleasing pastor focuses on his career, and paycheck, we have allowed sin to enter into the church.

For a short time, in my rebellious year, I attended a mega-church. Man, did I have great experiences. I felt good, it was all new to me. It was refreshing to see people have an experience. After a while, and when I got back right with God again, I realized that all I had there was a religious experience. There were no lives changing, there were no people coming to the Lord, the people were not even bringing their bibles to church, and they were believing everything that the pastors were saying.

In my opinion when a person does not bring their bible to church, they have no interest in that bible. I am not talking about the one that once in a while forgets their bible, I am talking about the one that doesn't see the need to bring the bible to church. The rejection of the things of God brings evil upon the things of man. The Lord is clear my dear pastor friend, now you, and you alone, must make your choice. Is this a career or a calling? If it is a calling then follow the Lord and let the chips fall where they may, if it is a career then do yourself a favor and resign. Remember that you, like myself, will have to answer to God for not obeying his call.

Jeremiah 7:1-7
The word that came to Jeremiah from the Lord, saying, 2. Stand in the gate of the Lord's house, and proclaim there this word, and say, Hear the word of the Lord, all ye of Judah, that enter in at these gates to worship the Lord. The Lord told Jeremiah to proclaim the WORD of the Lord not the program of the Lord. God told Jeremiah, the God-called pastor, to stand in the gates of the Lord's house and preach the word of the Lord. Where is the command to please men? Proclaiming the word of the Lord in the house of the Lord is to keep it holy, to keep the Lord in the middle of the church, it is to keep the Lord leading the pastor, to lead the church. A God-called pastor that is doing his job will always lead his people to the Lord, and not care about the approval of man.

3. Thus saith the Lord of hosts, the God of Israel, Amend your ways and your doings, and I will cause you to dwell in this place. The word of the Lord is telling the people to turn from their sins. God says that if they turn from their sins then he, God, will get all over that church, and then they can worship him. If the people amend their ways, if they repent of their wrong doings then the Lord can heal them, he can walk with them and then they will find that true life in Jesus.

A man-pleasing pastor, the best he can ever do, is lead people to himself, and his ways will never be able to be amended, repentance will never take place. It ALWAYS took the man of God, the God-called preacher, to proclaim the word of the Lord to see the people change. The one advantage that we have today is that the people now have the bible for themselves to read, study and to learn. However, if the man-pleasing pastor sees no importance in the word of God, then the people will never see the importance in the word of God.

4. Trust ye not in lying words, saying, The temple of the Lord, The temple of the Lord, The temple of the Lord, are these. 5. For if ye throughly amend your ways and your doings; if ye throughly execute judgment between a man and his neighbour; 6. If ye oppress not the stranger, the fatherless, and the widow, and shed not innocent blood in this place, neither walk after other gods to your hurt: 7. Then will I cause you to dwell in this place, in the land that I gave to your fathers, for ever and ever. My dear pastor friend, it does not get any more clear than this, if the word of God is preached, the programs are forsaken, the careers are rejected, the money is no longer a focus and the focus is on the God of the bible, the Lord will cause his people to dwell in his presence forever.

God has not now, nor ever will move from his position, it is man that makes that move. I challenge you my pastor friend, if you are reading this and are struggling in your role as a pastor, seek those old paths. If you are not a God-called pastor the Lord will show you on that old path, if you are seeking the programs, then amend your ways and get back to those old paths, there you will see God move in ways you never dreamed.

THE SOWER AND THE SEED

Psalm 126:6
He that goeth forth and weepeth, bearing precious seed, shall doubtless come again with rejoicing, bringing his sheaves with him.

In this chapter we will discuss two major points that will determine if a pastor will either leave the ministry or cleave to the ministry. Leaving the ministry for a pastor in my opinion, and based on examples in the bible, which shows that leaving the ministry should never be an option for a God-called pastor, however not everyone believes the same thing as I do. I have not come across one person in the bible that was called or used by God that quit, retired, or left his ministry. Yes, a couple of them may have done their ministry kicking and screaming (Jonah) but the men of God remained in their ministry until they reached eternity, and my dear pastor friend, I believe we are to do the same.

If a church offers you a retirement package, make it with the stipulation that they are ONLY to pay it out upon physically not being able to do the work of the ministry. In other words, if let's say, you had a stroke and are incapacitated and have to resign, then yes, that is one case. However, if God is using a man for himself, and that man is seeking God it is in God's hands, and he will do what is needed to provide for his man.

Quitting, let me say it nicer than that, looking forward to exiting your ministry, (retirement, quitting) should not even be considered for those called by God to the ministry. God's calling is not for a short time, it is for you to do for the rest of your life here on earth. We are to sow the seeds of the gospel. Yes, a lot of that seed will fall on many different types of ground, and most of it will not be received, however, we must sow that seed, and let God bring the results.

We are living in an age where the sower sows his seed on rocky ground then, stays there and tries to clean up that seed, and he ends up living in that condition teaching people not to focus on the seed but on the ground. The vision must be on the seed as the seed is the word, let that seed fall where it may and let God make it grow. Today we often spend so much time on the non-fertile ground trying to make the seed grow. Today's pastors spend time trying to remove the stones from the rocky ground, and try to dig, and dig, to get that ground to accept the seed, but at the same time, they are letting that seed get corrupt.

Simply put, I am saying that the pastors of today are spending way too much time trying to change the people, and their surroundings to make them feel good, or to attract them. In doing so, they must compromise the bible which creates the condition that many churches are in now. Our job is to sow, to plant, and water, it is God's job to bring the increase.

It is the job of the sower to sow that seed, it is not his job to change the seed, to limit the amount of seed that is planted, it is his job to spread that seed and let it grow where it grows, and leave what does not grow. When planting seed in a field, it is the ground that produces that fruit, but the seed is what germinates in that ground to produce certain fruit.

I could take a field and plow that field and go through and plant corn seed and after some time, some watering and sunlight that corn seed will germinate that ground and everywhere that seed was planted there most likely will be corn rising up. I can take that same ground, plow it and plant lettuce seed and that same field will produce lettuce fruit, it is the seed that germinates the field. The same is true with the word of God. This world is full of people that are the ground, if bad seeds are planted, the ground will produce bad fruit.

Man can be compared to the ground in this illustration by saying, he is the ground. If a man is focused in on sin, and lives without Jesus Christ as his Saviour, then he is only going to grow corrupt fruit, however, take that same man, plant the seed of the word of God, and the seed begins to germinate in him, this man begins to grow in Christ, he is now producing good fruit.

It Is the bible that produces that fruit, the bible tells us that we, us, mankind, will be known by OUR fruits,(Matthew 7:20) The word of God, the bible, is what germinated that fruit in our lives. If we sow corrupt seed, or the seed of these modern-day versions of the bible, that lead people away from the Lord, all we are doing is sowing the seed of Satan and driving people from the Lord.

We must focus on the truth of the seed, we as pastors must preach and teach the word for what it says, we must do it without apology, and we must never compromise that word or we are sowing a corrupt seed. It is the seed that tells the soil what to grow, the heart of man is that soil, it is the word of God that tells that man what to do, so our intentions and focus should be on Jesus, through his word in the bible. If you compromise the bible, if you as a pastor do not preach on hell, the lake of fire, sin, repentance, forgiveness, etc., you are sowing that corrupt seed as your focus is more on the ground than it is on that seed. Let the seed, the word of God, do its job, just go, and plant that seed. I am reminded of a passage that will fit this illustration, it is in John 4

John 4:34-38

Jesus saith unto them, My meat is to do the will of him that sent me, and to finish his work. The two main points of the Lord Jesus is to do God's will and to FINISH his work. That is a loaded statement, the first of which, to do the will of the Lord one MUST be in the will of the Lord. I understand that at times it may be hard to find the will of the Lord, but just get busy doing something for the Lord and he will direct you to the calling he has for you.

If you feel called to preach and you are not sure, get involved with the children's or nursing home ministries and work in those ministries. The Lord will provide opportunities for you to preach, if the church allows the men in the church to preach a message then preach, if the youth group needs a person to teach a Sunday school class then teach that class. As you do that preaching and teaching you will get more opportunities to do them, the more you do them the more the Lord will either confirm that call, or deny that call, and you will know for sure if you are in his will.

Now to the one that is in the will of the Lord, and fulfilling that calling, you, us, we, are to do his will until it is FINISHED. Finished simply defined is: *entirely done.* What a definition that is, to be entirely done means that for a pastor or a call into ministry we are not entirely done until we reach glory, this means that that truly God-called pastor will hold the course, he will stay in his ministry and he will endure the hardships until he is entirely done. The man-pleasing pastor will run at the first sound of difficulty, he will run at the thought of hardship and he is always looking for that exit plan either through retirement or running to many different churches. Folks, you God-called pastors, please stay the course, please do not quit, please do things God's way, and let him work it all out for you.

35. Say not ye, There are yet four months, and then cometh harvest? behold, I say unto you, Lift up your eyes, and look on the fields; for they are white already to harvest. Notice that the fields are already plowed, they have already been made ready. All we have to do is sow that seed, not to work the field but sow that seed. Jesus already made that field ready to receive the seed, he did that on Calvary he made salvation available to all who receive that seed, let the good seed fall, spread it everywhere and let it germinate where it will, the seed will grow where it needs to grow, that is the power of the word of God it needs no defense from me, it needs no help from me, it needs no approval from me, all it needs to do is to be planted, to be spread and then watered by going over it again, and again, and let it produce that good fruit.

Pastor, it is your job to spread that seed to your church, it is our job as Christians to sow that seed to the world. For the pastor it is crucial that you are sowing the truth, that the seed you are planting is the word of God that leads people back to him, it is not for you to change that seed, to reduce that seed, to not sow it because it may offend others, just plant it, because if you produce good fruit that will last and spread to many generations and that will be to your credit for the Lord. The same is also true if you sow that corrupt seed, and you compromise that seed and only sow bits and pieces of that seed, you will for generations to come reap that corruption of that planted corrupt seed, and yes, my dear pastor friend, that too will be credited to you.

Can you imagine standing before God and saying that you were more focused on what you could get out of the ministry, and didn't care about that seed, and didn't really care that you led people farther away from the Lord? I cannot even imagine how that will feel on that day of judgment.

36. And he that reapeth receiveth wages, and gathereth fruit unto life eternal: that both he that soweth and he that reapeth may rejoice together. The bible is clear here that if we sow our seeds, and we reap what we sow, we will receive our wages. Wages simply defined is*: payment*, if we do the work of the Lord we will receive payment from the Lord for doing his work. We may not have that fancy car, a mansion in the rich part of town, there may be times that we are not able to buy groceries, but make no mistake about it the Lord knows the need, and he is getting the reaping ready. We must work the field and reap that harvest.

That harvest for us is the lost people of this world, the hurting of this world, and the broken people of this world. We are to gather them together and get them to focus on Jesus as he is the only one that can change their lives. As we work our ministries, we witness, we preach, we teach, we listen, we pray, and as we seek God we begin to see people coming to church, we begin to see souls getting saved, we begin to see lives changing. Yes, it is God that makes those changes, however as the ones that labored we get to reap in the blessings of that.

My dear pastor friend, it is crucial that you hold the course, it is important that you do not quit your ministry, your little church needs you, keep working that ministry, keep bathing it in prayer and God will bring the people. Sometimes the people will come one at a time, sometimes many at a time. Keep working your ministry, to work a field to get the crop one must remain in that field until all the crop is picked, until the work is entirely done (finished). We are to work our ministries until they are entirely done, until they are finished.

37. And herein is that saying true, One soweth, and another reapeth. 38. I sent you to reap that whereon ye bestowed no labour: other men laboured, and ye are entered into their labours. Jesus is saying here that he has already laboured, he has already gotten that field ready to plant the gospel seed. All we have to do is plant then reap, he did the hard work. When he said we bestowed no labour, he meant that the plan of salvation was not a work that we could do. Jesus did that work on the cross, now all we have to do is to plant that seed, to preach the gospel, to get the people to fall in love with Jesus. The best way to get people to fall in love with Jesus is for you to be in love with him yourself. You must first love the Lord, and be seeking him, for you to be able to lead others to do the same thing.

I have found that the more I seek the Lord, the more honest and open I am with the people in the church, the more I show them I am like them, that I am a person that makes mistakes, that does not know everything about the bible, a person that is human, who truly loves the Lord, the more they begin to see my relationship with the Lord, the more they begin to want that same kind of a relationship.

Psalm 126:6

He that goeth forth and weepeth, bearing precious seed, shall doubtless come again with rejoicing, bringing his sheaves with him. When we go to do the will of the Lord we are not to do it half way with little to no effort, we are to do it with all our heart. This verse says that he that goeth forth and weepeth. When was the last time you wept for the people in your church? When was the last time that they worked against you that took them to the Lord in prayer, praying for them to follow the word of the Lord.

Pastors, we need to labour in prayer for our people, we need to weep for that seed of the gospel to reach the lost of the world. The lost people of the world are heading to hell very quickly, and we may just be that only Jesus they will see or hear. The world is a little different today than it was when I grew up. When I grew up, people were at least going to church, many people knew the importance of church but now, today, it is the church people that are no longer going to church.

It was much the same in bible times, in the days of Jesus and Paul. Many false teachings were out there, many rejected the gospel. But, many also got saved because that seed of the word of God was sown. The seed was spread by the men that poured their soul to God to be used by God. Most often that man was hated, he was put in jail, he was beaten, while still weeping for that seed to penetrate that hardened heart. Oh, What a Savior! Oh hallelujah! I am so glad that Jesus gave that seed, and because of his work on the cross, others got saved, and led my family to the Lord. They were bearing that precious seed with weeping.

The man-pleasing pastor that is looking for the larger salary, the "bigger church" can look all he wants. That man can seek for his retirement, and his large crowds but, he is not bearing that precious seed. The man-pleasing pastor will never receive the true victory for the Lord, he will never come again with rejoicing, he will never bring his sheaves with him. The man-pleasing pastor gets his reward now, the God-called pastor gets some reward here, but most of it up in glory. A pastor that can bring his sheaves with him is one that has discipled his people to follow Jesus. The God-called men are serving the Lord, and are bringing the sheaves with them. Sheave simply defined is*: a bundle of grain gathered after reaping.*

Mark 4:13-20

And he said unto them, Know ye not this parable? and how then will ye know all parables? 14. The sower soweth the word. There it is, the SOWER soweth the WORD. We, as Christians, not just pastors, are the Sowers. We are the ones that are to spread the gospel to the lost and dying world. We are the ones that are to show the love of Christ to others so that the Lord can be glorified. The bible asks here; do we not know this? Jesus is also asking his disciples here; Do you not know that you are the sower?

As pastors, our job is to sow the word of God to our sheep, those that the Lord has allowed to be under our responsibility as well as those that go to our churches, and the surrounding churches. It is crucial that we remember this. We are to lead the people in sowing the seed. If the leader, the pastor, does not lead people to Christ, most likely the people will have no desire to see Christ either. If the pastor is a God-called pastor, he will always sow the seed of Christ even to the saved. The seed goes beyond salvation; that seed can be in righteous living as well. The man-pleasing pastor just will not care and will only focus on himself.

15. And these are they by the way side, where the word is sown; but when they have heard, Satan cometh immediately, and taketh away the word that was sown in their hearts. The way side here, is the side of the road or the side of a path. The wayside is the part that is all gravel and no soil is present. This parable refers to four different types of land that the seed will fall on. Whichever soil the seed falls on, will determine the strength of the growth of the word. The quality of the soil will determine how well that seed takes.

When we sow the gospel to the world some will hear it, some will receive it, and some will reject it. The people that will receive it, will show what type of soil they have by how well the seed is rooted in them. This first type of seed has been sown but only heard and not fully received. This is like when you plant grass seed or spread fertilizer. If you are using a broadcast spreader, you will have some of that seed on the sidewalk or the road, that seed is spread but then it can get swept away. The first type is referring to the seed that never hits the soil, it was only seen by a person and not received.

In this passage the seed is the word, so the word of God is preached, it is taught, it is heard, but then immediately Satan comes with the broom to sweep that seed away. Satan, or his messengers, come to tell the people a false gospel, or false doctrines, we see this everywhere today. Satan is waitin' to remove that seed from anyone that he can.

16. And these are they likewise which are sown on stony ground; who, when they have heard the word, immediately receive it with gladness; 17. And have no root in themselves, and so endure but for a time: afterward, when affliction or persecution ariseth for the word's sake, immediately they are offended. Stony ground, this is the most common ground that the word of God is sown on today. Many people today receive the word, they will get on board with the bible and start living for the Lord, but their roots are weak. Have you ever planted a garden, or seen flower beds? Once in a while, around the rocks, in that bed there are weeds growing from the rock because some dirt got built up on the rock. It takes just a small amount of effort to pull that weed out. This is the example the second type of soil is referring to.

Those people who have the word sown on rocky ground, will come to church, they will bring their bible however, they will not engage in any bible reading at their house, or in their personal time, they will not have that one-on-one time with the Lord. These people have the word sown on rocky ground, and are the ones that will do all the right stuff for the Lord, you will have the confidence in their relationship with God, but the moment something goes wrong, and my friend, things do go wrong, they get offended and quit. The reason they quit is because the seed, the word of God, had no root in them. Notice here in this verse it says that they have no root in themselves, in other words they did not seek the things of the bible they only let what they heard in church be their guide.

18. And these are they which are sown among thorns; such as hear the word, 19. And the cares of this world, and the deceitfulness of riches, and the lusts of other things entering in, choke the word, and it becometh unfruitful. These are today's Christians. The ones that the bible in the book of Romans calls carnal Christians. These Christians love the things of the world probably more than they love the Lord. These are the ones that are saved, but are only concerned about their own salvation, and nothing else. These carnal Christians will get mad at the preacher for preaching against sin because it affects the sin that is in their lives, they will be the ones that sow discord among the brethren because of the sins that they love so much.

The Christians that still hold on to the things of the world, these are the thorns that choke out the word.

Yes, the seed gets in there, and it grows, but it grows among the thorns, and the thorns always choke out the good. Every gardener knows that anytime there is good seed mixed in with the thorns, the thorns always win. These folks become unfruitful, they in essence will hinder the work of the Lord, they will be the ones that only show up for church but nothing else, they are the everyday Christians.

Carnal Christians will make everything else in their lives a priority over the things of the Lord. You can always tell, because they will be able to do anything, and everything else in their lives, but when it comes to the things of the Lord, they always have some excuse. They are too sick for church but, healthy enough for that ball game. Pastors, it is our responsibility to sow that seed, and sow it everywhere, the Lord grows the seed we are only to plant, water and reap.

20. And these are they which are sown on good ground; such as hear the word, and receive it, and bring forth fruit, some thirtyfold, some sixty, and some an hundred. Now we get to the good ground! Notice out of the four different grounds mentioned there are three that hinder the roots and the growth of the seed. This shows us that only one-fourth of the seed planted will grow correctly, but that growth will be a strong growth, it will be a lasting growth. That good ground Christian will be fully surrendered to the things of the Lord, they will seek him in their personal lives, they will seek him in their family lives, they will seek him in every area of their lives, and in everything they do.

Pastors this is what makes the ministry we are in worth it all. The one-fourth keeps us going. God-called pastors seek for that good ground while the man-pleasing pastors seek that other ground. Let them seek that other ground. My dear God-called pastor friend, if God has truly called you, and you have the power of the Lord in your church the bible will do one of two things, it will either drive people away from the church in rebellion, or it will drive people closer to God in repentance.

Keep sowing that seed! We as pastors, must fast, pray, seek the Lord beseeching him to do what he can. The seed at times, will be hard to sow, it will be hard to tell people that they are wretched, miserable sinners that need Jesus. However, we must let the seed fall where it may, it will not be a total loss, there will be some that will receive it. My friend, keep sowing the seed of the gospel, it is crucial. the God-called pastor that is cleaving to his call, and his ministry will understand this. The man-pleasing pastor will be like the seed sown on stony ground, when the trials come they quit.

Matthew 13:37-43

He answered and said unto them, He that soweth the good seed is the Son of man; 38. The field is the world; the good seed are the children of the kingdom; but the tares are the children of the wicked one; Jesus highlights the seed and the sower. The one that sows the good seed, the one that brought the gospel to the world is Jesus Christ. Jesus delivered the gospel to the world through his shed blood, this is the good seed. We that are saved are the ones that are continuing the work of the Lord. We are the ones that are telling others about the Lord, we are the ones that have that broken heart for the lost, the field is the world.

The Lord has already plowed the field, Jesus did the work on the cross. It is time to plant that seed, let it root where it roots, and let the Lord do what he will do with it. The tares in the world are the weeds. Tares simply defined is*: a weed; an undesirable element.* The tares are the weeds that try to choke out the seed. We must continue to sow that seed no matter the difficulty.

39. The enemy that sowed them is the devil; the harvest is the end of the world; and the reapers are the angels. This verse says a lot. The tares are from the seeds that are sown from the Devil. The devil will always plant the tares in the field to try and get rid of the seed. The seed of the gospel draws people to the Lord, the seed of tares draws people to the Devil. The harvest is the end of the world. The good seeds will produce those that step into eternity going to heaven. As we reap those fields, as we bring our sheaves with us, we will rejoice in the victories of souls coming to Jesus Christ.

This verse outlines our enemy. This verse shows us that for as many seeds as we sow, there will be as many as tares sown also. Satan is working against us in every aspect of the process. But, I am often reminded of I John 4:4 where the bible says, greater is the Lord that is in us, than Satan that is in the world. If we keep that verse in mind my dear friend, it will be an encouragement. We need to continue to move forward for the cause of the Lord. It is the ones that quit at the hardships that in actuality are working for Satan. Though that is not their intent, it is what they are doing. Please, my dear pastor friend, cleave to your ministry, do not leave it, you have come this far, keep going the victory will come, and when it comes, Oh man, you will be able to rejoice in the Lord knowing it was the Lord that did it.

40. As therefore the tares are gathered and burned in the fire; so shall it be in the end of this world. At the end the tares, those that reject the Lord, those that work for Satan will be gathered, and burned. The tares will end up in the lake of fire being tormented for all eternity, they will never be destroyed. Our job as pastors is to let the people know that if they are tares that destruction is surely waiting for them, but if they turn to Jesus they will have eternal life in heaven with the Lord. Oh, how the tares have destroyed the church today that the Lord has built. There was a time when the church would reject the tares, but now they are allowing them to stay, the tares are the ones that know better. Lukewarm Christians are just as bad as the lost in some ways, because neither group seeks the Lord.

41. The Son of man shall send forth his angels, and they shall gather out of his kingdom all things that offend, and them which do iniquity; 42. And shall cast them into a furnace of fire: there shall be wailing and gnashing of teeth. At the end, at the judgment, Jesus will gather all those that are not his, all those that have rejected him, and will have them thrown into the lake of fire. Jesus will separate the tares from his children. Oh, what a day that will be! These tares that think they will be ok at the judgment but they will be reminded of the times they rejected the Lord. On that day they will say. "Ok Lord! now I believe." just to save themselves, but it will be too late. The bible says that there will be weeping and wailing and gnashing of teeth. Wailing simply defined is: *to cry out loud*. Gnashing simply defined is: *to strike or grind*. There will be people grinding their teeth, and crying out loud because they have to face the reality of their decisions to reject Jesus

43. Then shall the righteous shine forth as the sun in the kingdom of their Father. Who hath ears to hear, let him hear. The good seed will take root and shine forth at the end. The bible says, he that hath ears let him hear. It is crucial that we keep sowing the seed of the gospel. We may not see the results now, but one day we will. We may be in glory before we see the results of the seed we have sown, God's word, but we need to keep going, to keep working. All that quitting has ever accomplished is to hurt people, anger people, and discourage people. Quitting has never produced effective people for the Lord.

Quitting not only makes the people discouraged, it makes them lose hope in the Lord.
This also makes the pastor quit, never to grow for the Lord, and never accomplish for the Lord those that those that the men that held the course could do. It is not the man, it is the Lord that brings the results, but he does it through those that follow him, for those that do not quit. What if when the children of Israel got to the promised land and sent the twelve spies to see the land, if they listened not to the ten that said it was too difficult to do this and we need to just quit, but listened to the two that said we can take this land. Where would we be today?

Galatians 6:6-9
Let him that is taught in the word communicate unto him that teacheth in all good things. 7. Be not deceived; God is not mocked: for whatsoever a man soweth, that shall he also reap. This should be a wake-up verse for the God-called pastor. The verse tells us we must sow the truth even when it is

not popular, we must sow the truth even when it hurts to do so because, if we do not sow the truth we will not reap the reward of truth. If Christians sow corrupt seed, we will reap a corrupt fruit.

For the man-pleasing pastor this should be a verse that tells them to quit, and find what God has for them to do or to repent, and get right with God. The longer they are in the ministry for themselves, the more corruption they sow and their judgment will be deeper. They will have to be held more accountable for the corrupt selfish fruit they are sowing. We MUST sow the truth of the seed of the gospel so we can reap what the Lord has grown, so we can be known by our fruits.

8. For he that soweth to his flesh shall of the flesh reap corruption; but he that soweth to the Spirit shall of the Spirit reap life everlasting. Man-pleasing pastors will reap man-pleasing results. God-called pastors will reap God blessed results. The difference is the man-pleasing pastor that quits at every turn, will sow corruption, he will sow the seeds of pride, and lust, and that will be his fruit. He that sows to the flesh SHALL of the flesh reap CORRUPTION.

God-called pastors will labor in prayer, they will fast, they will do all they can for the people in their fold. The God-called pastor will self-sacrifice and trust that God will do what he can do. They will cleave to their calling, hold the course, they will endure the hardships, and they will grow in the Lord in ways they had never thought possible. The God-called man knows that sowing the seeds of righteousness will cause him to reap the fruits of righteousness. They that sow to the Spirit, will reap life everlasting. Oh, what a Savior, Oh Hallelujah.

9. And let us not be weary in well doing: for in due season we shall reap, if we faint not. God-called pastors know this to be true. We SHALL reap if we do not quit, when the going gets tough. If we stay the course, we hold the line, we continue to do the work, it is then that we will reap the fruit, it may not come right away but, it will come

The man-pleasing pastor wants results now, they want their churches filled now. When the church does not fill up immediately, they say, "The people do not want the Lord." So they go to the next church, and to the next, never waiting on the Lord. I had a mindset like this for quite a while, until the Lord took me to Colorado. We were all alone, my wife and I, doing the ministry. I was of the mindset that when things went wrong that it was the people, instead of realizing that it was me, or that we were the problem. I was determined to find God's will for my life, I was resolved in my efforts to seek him.

It was when I got to Bethel, where I pastor now, that the Lord showed me why I had to go to Colorado, why I had to learn to endure through two years with only one person coming to church. I figured we would plant a church, a little on the compromising side. If we relaxed the music standards the people would come. But, it was not until I began to preach the bible for what it said, regardless of the number of people that came to church, that the Lord worked on my heart. The Lord began to show me whether I was a God-called or man-pleasing pastor.

God cannot use man-pleasing pastors. God had to separate me from myself, and my ideas so he could use me in the ministry, so he could make me what I need to be for him. Pastors do not quit, do not jump churches. I don't care if most of the people are against you, pray for them, labor for them, weep for them, fast for them, preach the truth of the bible, and let God sort it out. In a group of people that don't like a pastor, it is almost always one or two people in the group that stir up the others. When the Lord drives the tares out, the rest will stop resisting, and begin to get on board with the things of God.

ENDURING HARDSHIPS

2 Timothy 2:3
Thou therefore endure hardness, as a good soldier of Jesus Christ.

Endure simply defined is: *to remain firm under suffering*. When we think about this word and this definition, it opens a new outlook on the words "enduring hardships" in ministry and in our walk with God. The only way that one is ever going to grow, or to understand any of the true grace of God, other than salvation, is for them to stand strong through the hardships. This is where it gets difficult for many people, especially for the pastors of today, when hardships approach. Often people are not strong enough, they have not grown enough, or their faith is too weak to handle the difficulty, so they leave for the next best thing. They say. "Well, I have done all I can and the Lord is moving me."

People in this kind of a mindset, who always remain in this mindset, and never grow in the Lord, will never be successful for the Lord. Take any independent Baptist church that has had people coming for many years, and the attendance is faithful, and solid, and you will see a church that has remained firm during the suffering.

The bible tells us that suffering is coming for us as Christians. The bible says that all that live godly in Christ Jesus shall SUFFER persecution. (II Timothy 3:12) the bible also tells us that we, as Christians, are accounted as sheep for the slaughter. (Romans 8:36) Christians will suffer hardships and persecutions.

Suffering through these hardships is what makes people grow and get stronger through the Lord, it is what makes people grow in intimacy with the Lord, it is what makes them understand on a deeper level the love that God has for them. When a man of God, or a child of God learns to stand and remain firmly fixed through the difficult times, there is ALWAYS a great victory at the end.

How many wars in our history have ever been won without having to endure hardships? None. All successful things, wars, business, relationships, ministry, whatever is successful is because those involved dealt with the difficulties, endured the hardships, shed many tears, they felt those hard hearts, they wept for the loss of a person. People continue on through difficult illnesses. Whatever the hardship we as the children of God will face, in that moment, we will make our choice to either leave or cleave to the God we serve in the ministry.

If quitting is not an option for you, and my dear friend I pray it is not, then you will learn to cleave to the ministry that God has given you. If quitting is an option for you, then you will leave the ministry, and never be successful for the Lord. There is ALWAYS grace from God during those hardships. I have seen this every time that we endure, there is a nugget of grace somewhere.

Let's say that there was an exodus in your church, people have left because you stood true to the bible. That loss of people in your church is hurting you. But then, after a couple of weeks, a visitor shows up that loves the fact that you stand strong for the bible. Others slowly come, that grace is always there, it is God showing you that he still has your back, that you must suffer through but he will comfort and strengthen you.

The men in the bible did not become men of God because they refused to endure their hardships. Look at Job, he was one that lost everything. Job lost property, people, and wealth but he endured that hardship, and kept on for the Lord. He was more blessed by God in the end than many others were as a result of staying faithful to God in his hardships.

When we see the examples set before us in the bible, we see that men like king David, who had to fight many battles. David endured loss of life, he had times of difficulty in his family, he wept for the people in his kingdom, but he kept going. Then we see the apostles who were beaten, put in prison, and John the Baptist gave his life when he had his head removed. Did these people recant their belief in God? Did they deny the Lord to their accusers? (Peter did, but then got right with God) Did these men quit when they were thrown in prison after being whipped in the streets for preaching the gospel? No, they did not, they endured their hardships. You, and I could have that same opportunity to receive strength from the Lord as they did. If those men had quit, if they had stopped their ministries the first time that someone hurt them, we might not have churches today.

Pastor, your people will at some point get mad at you, some will want you gone, some will stir up trouble against you, you have to make a choice, either to leave, or to stand and fight, enduring the hatred, the anger, the deception, understanding that greater is he (Jesus) that is in you than he (Satan) that is in the world. It is during these times my dear pastor friend, that you must take some time for yourself and get alone with God. These times when you get alone with God, will determine what kind of a pastor you are. Are you a man that God can use, or one that when your faith is tested, that it cannot be trusted.

I read a statement, that simply says, "a tested faith, is a trusted faith" Oh, how true that is. The problem in this modern age, and with this mindset, is that no one wants to be tested, so they quit. The result is seen in what we have today, there are men that run from the difficulties, that are always looking for the bigger, and better, their next best thing, that want to retire, men that are always looking for their "exit plan" from the ministry. These men are leading people to themselves and not to the Lord. Because men refuse to stand the course, the churches of today are just making people feel good and not seeing lives changed and souls getting saved.

As always, in all my books, let's not take my word for it, let's go to the bible directly. I pray that you never take what I write, in any of my books, as fact. I pray that you compare everything that I say to the word of God and let the Holy Spirit lead you to the truth. I am just a saved man, prone to make mistakes, sharing what I have learned over the years through studying the bible, and biblical principles. Please do not replace the bible with what I say here, please do not read this then go and preach a message from it. Search the bible for yourself, and get your understanding from the word of God.

2 Timothy 2:1-5
Thou therefore, my son, be strong in the grace that is in Christ Jesus. 2. And the things that thou hast heard of me among many witnesses, the same commit thou to faithful men, who shall be able to teach others also. Paul is telling Timothy to commit the truth of God to faithful men, in other words, to teach, and train those that are seeking God so they also can teach others. When we focus on the bible, and we make the bible the final authority in our lives, we can teach others.

We will never be able to teach others if we never learn to endure. Think about the times in church when you were going through a tough time in your life, and an older, and wiser person told you just hold a little longer that God has the solution worked out. I used to hate that when people would say, "God will meet the need." Enduring and trusting God when the rent is three days past due, the car doesn't work, or the bills are piling up is the kind of hardship that teaches a person to trust God in all things.

I would listen to those older folks and think, well they don't know what they are talking about, it is easy for them to say that because they have money to pay their bills, they have food to eat, they have a working car. What I failed to understand, at that time, is that at some point in their lives, they too had to endure their own hardships. It was during the time of enduring their own hardships that they learned to trust God and now they, are trying to teach others to do the same.

This is what Paul is saying here, by enduring the hardships, you will begin to see God work through them, and you will learn to draw closer to God and be more at peace with things that are happening because of those hardships. You will NEVER learn the power of God without enduring the hardships, you will NEVER grow in your walk with God without enduring the hardships.

3. Thou therefore endure hardness, as a good soldier of Jesus Christ. Paul understood hardness, he understood that people will not receive the gospel, he understood that people would hate him because he told them the truth. Paul understood that enduring hardships is part of spreading the gospel. I mean, just go outside, and share the gospel with people. You will see how much they hate the message, and as a matter of fact, you will see that many carnal Christians will hate that same message.

Paul, because has endured these hardships, has the authority to encourage Timothy to do the same. Paul has the experience of being beaten, whipped, stoned almost to death, all for souls to get saved. But for Paul it is even greater to have God's glory on him and his message. At the end of the day, the worst thing that hardship could ever do is to send us to see the Saviour if someone were to kill us for the faith.

4. No man that warreth entangleth himself with the affairs of this life; that he may please him who hath chosen him to be a soldier. 5. And if a man also strive for masteries, yet is he not crowned,

except he strive lawfully. Simply put, a man that is seeking any kind of a reward will only receive that true reward if he does it the right way.

I understand that no one wants to endure the hardships, I get it, I really do, I spent many years running from those hardships, and even now I don't want to go through them. In the years I spent running from those hardships, I never grew in my walk with God, I remained in that carnal, self-serving state that never did anyone, especially me, any good. However, I am no longer running from the hardships of serving the Lord, and am walking with the Lord through them because I see the crown at the end.

I know the reward that will come, and I am beginning to see the power of the Lord on my life. We are seeing prayers answered, we are seeing lives change, we are seeing souls coming to Jesus, all because we no longer want to cheat to get the crown. We are now ready to earn it the correct way no matter how difficult it may be. We are beginning to see the church grow.

2 Thessalonians 1:1-5
Paul, and Silvanus, and Timotheus, unto the church of the Thessalonians in God our Father and the Lord Jesus Christ: 2. Grace unto you, and peace, from God our Father and the Lord Jesus Christ. 3. We are bound to thank God always for you, brethren, as it is meet, because that your faith groweth exceedingly, and the charity of every one of you all toward each other aboundeth; 4. So that we ourselves glory in you in the churches of God for your patience and faith in all

your persecutions and tribulations that ye endure: Paul is commending this church for them enduring through the difficult times. Notice it says that their patience and faith increases as a result of endurance.

I have maintained through this book that pastors who quit and do not hold course are man-pleasing and not God-called pastors. A God-called pastor will endure so his faith will increase. The bible tells us that faith comes by hearing, and hearing by the word of God. (Romans 10:17) If we, as pastors, are not willing to hold the course, if all we want is a crown that we did not earn but, cheated to get it by not enduring the hardships, all the fruit can ever possibly come from such a ministry is of self-pleasing people who have a form of godliness but, but denies the power thereof. (II Timothy 3:5) Remember my dear pastor friend, you, like I, will have to stand before the same God and have to answer for the same things. What will you say to God when he asks why you quit?

Endurance builds patience, it increases faith, it grows your relationship with God, it furthers your convictions, it allows you to understand bible level Christianity that the prophets of old had, and the power that they received from God as a result. Anyone can change programs in a church and apply smoke and fancy lights to their services. Anyone can have a rock band lead a "worship" service, anyone can soften up sin and repentance. Anyone can make their service geared toward emotional experiences, but it is the God-called pastor who will never let his church get to that point. The God-called pastor's job is to keep the church holy, and without blame, so God can change lives and souls can be saved. Folks, it is all about God, not about us.

Will people be able to see your walk with God as an example to follow? Will people generations from now, if the Lord tarries, be able to say I want a ministry like that man had. Will you be that person? Or, will your fruit only last while you are here, and in church, after church, because you have never found that peace from God that ONLY comes from enduring the hardships?

5. Which is a manifest token of the righteous judgment of God, that ye may be counted worthy of the kingdom of God, for which ye also suffer: For a man of God to be counted worthy he MUST endure hardships. This verse is plain and simple. To be counted worthy for the ministry to which we are called, we will have to suffer through and endure those hardships even when, and especially when, they hurt. The hardships will make you question your very walk with God, hardships will make you question God's love for you. Hardships will make you doubt, and face decisions like never before. But, as the bible says, we will face temptations, but there is ALWAYS a way of escape from those temptations. When you are in the middle of the worst suffering of your life, and God shows up for you, Oh, man, what an experience, what a faith builder that is. What victory you will win and crowns you will receive because you endured through the hardships and were found faithful.

Remember the three Hebrew boys in the furnace? It was when they were in the furnace, that God showed up. What about Daniel? Daniel had to be in the lion's den, then God showed up. What about David? David had to be running toward the giant, then God showed up. These men of God did not quit, they endured through the pain and suffering, possibly questioning

God in some instances, but they knew, in their hearts, that they were not to quit, and they received the victory. Because they endured, they received a deeper relationship with God, they achieved that bible level Christianity.

2 Timothy 2:10

Therefore I endure all things for the elect's sakes, that they may also obtain the salvation which is in Christ Jesus with eternal glory. Paul says here that he endures ALL things so he can get the gospel out to others. See folks, if there is no meat (bible truth) in what you are saying, there will never be a result from the work. Think of it like this, no one has ever suffered persecution for a lie, no one has ever endured torture, death, loss of family for something that is a lie. When we endure the hardships it puts the power of God behind the message of the cross. What if Jesus himself never went to the cross? What kind of saving power would there have been in his death? What if he had just died of natural causes? Christianity would have ended right there. I cannot speak for anyone else, but for me I want the fruit of the gospel in my life. I am planning to remain strong for the many generations that come long after I am dead and in glory.

2 Timothy 3:10-12

But thou hast fully known my doctrine, manner of life, purpose, faith, longsuffering, charity, patience, 11. Persecutions, afflictions, which came unto me at Antioch, at Iconium, at Lystra; what persecutions I endured: but out of them all the Lord delivered me. Paul goes on here to tell Timothy that the Lord delivered him out of his afflictions. Paul was delivered by God, who walked with him while he was enduring persecution and hardship, because he was looking forward to the end result. The end result of our suffering, enduring that suffering, and not quitting, is for the sake of the gospel. We messengers will receive rewards in glory for our faithfulness but, the rewards we receive are for the sake of the gospel, and for the glory of God.

Timothy knew the doctrine that Paul was preaching. Almost every one that quits the ministry, as a man-pleasing pastor knows the doctrines, they know the manner of life of those before them who were teaching them. They are aware of the faith and charity and afflictions, but they have not endured. Though they know all of these things, they do not have the faith to see it through. If they just hold the course, and endure the faith will come.

The bible tells us in I Corinthians 4:2 that is REQUIRED of a STEWARD (we as Christians, we as pastors) to be found FAITHFUL. Being faithful means we are to endure so our faith will increase. The bible is a living and powerful book that leads you to God through Jesus Christ, and it is amazing how everything ties into the same theme. We must endure to receive the victory.

12. Yea, and all that will live godly in Christ Jesus shall suffer persecution. At the end of this passage it says YES, ALL that will live godly in Christ Jesus SHALL suffer persecution. If you are going to do the work of a pastor you must be willing to do it God's way or it will be all about you, and not about God. If you are going to have a holy and acceptable ministry for the Lord you must suffer afflictions, persecutions, you must endure, and still keep going through it all, or else you will never be able to accomplish anything for the Lord. All you will ever do is be "always learning but NEVER able to come to the knowledge of truth." (II Timothy 3:7)

2 Timothy 4:1-8
I charge thee therefore before God, and the Lord Jesus Christ, who shall judge the quick and the dead at his appearing and his kingdom; 2. Preach the word; be instant in season, out of season; reprove, rebuke, exhort with all longsuffering and doctrine. The way to get that endurance, is to preach the word without apology. A man-pleasing pastor will never make the preaching the main focus in his ministry, he will always make the attendance numbers, and the money the main focus. The world, and carnal Christians, do not like the truth of the bible, so if they limit it, or remove it, they are happy because they are glorifying their sin and blaming it on God. Not only do the lost and carnal Christians blame God but now, the pastors are doing the same thing. These churches that are not making God a priority, began because the leader of the church, the pastor, at some point stopped serving God, and making God the priority, and focused on serving himself.

My dear friend, PREACH THE WORD, let the chips fall where they may. You are not held accountable for another person's walk with God, that is between the individual and the Lord. However, you are held accountable to God for not preaching and teaching the truth. You will be held accountable to God for not enduring. Preach the word, endure the hardships because the next few verses explain why you must endure.

3. For the time will come when they will not endure sound doctrine; but after their own lusts shall they heap to themselves teachers, having

itching ears; 4. And they shall turn away their ears from the truth, and shall be turned unto fables. Man-pleasing pastors have allowed this to happen. We live in times that people will not endure sound doctrine, so they vote in their own pastors, and give them large salaries. But, my friend, we cannot allow these changes at the expense of compromising the bible.

If you are a pastor reading this, and are truly trying to be a pastor that God has called, and are preaching in a compromising church, I exhort you to preach the word the next time you have that opportunity. Be prayed up, get the Holy Spirit all over it, most likely they will ask you to leave once you are done, but you never know what God will do in that case. If the church has you leave, that's okay. There are plenty of other churches that need pastors and there are many churches looking for God-called pastors to lead them. Yes, they are all small, but preach the word and let the word of God build God's church. It takes time, effort, and endurance to see the result. You are better off to obey God in preaching the word than to be an "ear tickler." You will be held accountable before God either way.

Remember, YOU, not your elder board, not your church congregation, YOU, and YOU alone, will be held accountable to the God of the bible for how you lead your church. If the church will not endure sound doctrine, let the word of God drive them out, if they will endure sound doctrine let the word of God draw them in, either way, be the God-called pastor like the men of old. Let God do now what he did back then and endure the hardships, the victories are so worth it.

5. But watch thou in all things, endure afflictions, do the work of an evangelist, make full proof of thy ministry. Enduring the afflictions, the persecutions, the hardships are all part of making full proof of the ministry. Enduring the afflictions is what makes the ministry complete. There are hardships in anything that is worth doing, in relationships, in buildings, in business but, working through those hardships allows one to become wiser, more focused on the God of the bible and helps one remain solid in their walk with God, so that the enemy cannot get in.

Notice the order of statement in this verse. Paul is telling Timothy that while he is enduring the afflictions that he is to do the work of an evangelist, he is not to stop, he is not to quit, he is to do the work while enduring. All the pastors of old, that have been in the same churches for years, have all had their enduring to do, and have all had to do the work of the ministry while enduring. All who endured had victories in the end.

6. For I am now ready to be offered, and the time of my departure is at hand. 7. I have fought a good fight, I have finished my course, I have kept the faith: 8. Henceforth there is laid up for me a crown of righteousness, which the Lord, the righteous judge, shall give me at that day: and not to me only, but unto all them also that love his appearing. We should have that same response when it is our time to step into glory. Like Paul, we should be able to say, I have fought a good fight, meaning I have preached the word, I did not compromise, I did not waver in my belief. I have finished my course, meaning I have held the course, I have endured the hardships and the afflictions, I have kept going even when I wanted to quit or felt the weight of the world on my shoulders. Paul says in the last statement here, that he has kept the faith, there is only one way to keep the faith and that is to stay in the bible, endure the hardships, to endure the trials and be tested so that way you can hold the course, and keep the faith.

Hebrews 12:1-2
Wherefore seeing we also are compassed about with so great a cloud of witnesses, let us lay aside every weight, and the sin which doth so easily beset us, and let us run with patience the race that is set before us, 2. Looking unto Jesus the author and finisher of our faith; who for the joy that was set before him endured the cross, despising the shame, and is set down at the right hand of the throne of God. The bible tells us here that there are many examples for us to follow in the Christian faith. "so great a cloud of witnesses" this says that men and women ahead of us endured until the end, they did not quit, they did not look for the bigger or better, they kept on. Many of them kept on until death, they clave to their ministries, they did not leave them.

Our focus needs to be on Jesus, his reward needs to be the goal at the end of the race. In I Corinthians 9:24 we are told that to win the prize we must run the race. We must stay in the race, jumping over the hurdles that come so we can obtain the prize. The prize for those of us that are saved is, eternity with the Lord. Our goal on earth is to please the Father, and ultimately to be given rewards for selfless service for the Lord. We are to look to Jesus at the finish line.

God-called pastors will run the race, they may occasionally trip over the hurdles, but they get back up and keep going until the race is won. If a person never finishes anything in ministry, nothing will ever be accomplished. The man-pleasing pastor will stop before even jumping that hurdle, and he will leave the race, and look for the next one.

I understand quitting, and not finishing, I really do. I was once in that kind of a mindset when I was doing things for myself. I was living in my carnal life, my focus was only partially on Jesus, and a lot on myself. During the carnal stage of my life, I started a church. After about four months the church failed because I had my intentions and my goals in mind and not the Lord's intentions and goals. After I quit the church, I blamed God for it. I praise God, he gave me the opportunity to get right with him. I used to hear a saying when I was growing up, "winners never quit, and quitters never win." Oh, how true this little statement has proven to be. Pastors, we put so much work into the ministry. Why would anyone want to put that much work into it, just to have it all fall apart because they focused on themselves, and not the Lord?

James 1:12
Blessed is the man that endureth temptation: for when he is tried, he shall receive the crown of life, which the Lord hath promised to them that love him. Temptations can be those bigger, and better things, or desires. Temptation simply defined is: *a cause of enticement*. The Ministry has a lot of bigger, and better things that are enticing, for anyone. Now if the Lord calls a pastor to a bigger and better ministry then he must obey that call. However, the circumstances will be much different than just desiring bigger and better, and you will know it is from God.

God will not call a person to another ministry and let what they are doing for him now fail. If I am pastoring a church, and it is growing, and souls are getting saved, and the Lord wants me to move to another church, he will raise up someone that can take over my current position and keep it running so there is no loss in the current ministry. I don't see anywhere in the bible where the Lord moves a man, and sacrifices what he was initially doing that was blessing the Lord to another place.

The bible says that we are blessed if we endure temptation. Temptation comes in many sizes, and forms, it comes in the form of greed, envy, covetousness, pride, and many others things. If we endure those temptations and stand firm, we will be blessed by God. The bible not only says that we will be blessed but we will receive a crown of life for holding the course, we will receive the reward for completing the race. Those that quit will never receive those rewards, and they must still stand in the judgment before the Lord.

James 5:10-11
Take, my brethren, the prophets, who have spoken in the name of the Lord, for an example of suffering affliction, and of patience. We are to look to the men and women of the past who gave their lives, took the beatings, were burned and tortured all for the sake of the gospel. These people could have quit at any time, they could have just stopped preaching, and teaching, they could have just "retired" from the ministry and lived a peaceful life. But no, they knew whom they believed in, they knew the saviour, their faith was strong all because they clave to their ministries and did not run from them. In any persecution situation, I would stack up any truly bible

believing pastor against twenty modern day man-pleasing pastors. I guarantee that the God-called pastor will hold the course, and endure the temptation. The man-pleasing pastors will run, hide, and quit. The man-pleasing pastor leaves his ministry but the God-called pastor cleaves to his ministry.

Persecution, affliction, suffering, and enduring all these things builds patience in a person, it increases their faith, and bible convictions immensely. Struggles make them stronger. It is that endurance that God uses to build his churches, to build his people, to build things for himself.

11. Behold, we count them happy which endure. Ye have heard of the patience of Job, and have seen the end of the Lord; that the Lord is very pitiful, and of tender mercy. These folks that endured their trials and testing. They were counted as happy, they had a joy of the Lord that not many get to experience, they have a joy that only a few have ever truly felt. They had that intimate, personal walk with God that only those that endure hardships, and temptations can ever experience. Oh, what a Saviour, Oh hallelujah! Enduring the hardships and afflictions brings true joy to a Christian, it moves that bible-believing Christian to that higher bible level Christianity.

1 Peter 1:25 KJV
But the word of the Lord endureth for ever. And this is the word which by the gospel is preached unto you. The word of the Lord, the gospel message endures forever. If you think about it for a moment, the gospel has been a message that many men, and women over the years have tried to suppress. Many have tried to eliminate the gospel.

The bible today is banned in many countries, it is being listed as a fairy tale, it is hated by many nations, yet it keeps going. It has survived book burnings, it has survived persecutions, wars, peace times, you name it. Throughout history the bible has survived, it has endured through all this time. The word of God has endured and been tested and found faithful. If we are truly bible believers, we hold to that old bible, we will also endure through those hard times.

1 Peter 2:19-25
For this is thankworthy, if a man for conscience toward God endure grief, suffering wrongfully. 20. For what glory is it, if, when ye be buffeted for your faults, ye shall take it patiently? but if, when ye do well, and suffer for it, ye take it patiently, this is acceptable with God. The bible says if a person makes bad choices, or commits sins and suffers for their sins, it is a justified suffering, their suffering is deserved because of sinful actions. That kind of suffering is not considered enduring for the Lord, that is enduring your consequences for sinful behavior. But, the person that suffers for doing right will be blessed by God, they are the ones that are happy that the Lord found them worthy to suffer for him.

Growing up in church, I heard it said many times, those that suffered for the Lord counted not themselves worthy to suffer, they were happy that the Lord allowed them to suffer for him. I could never understand that until I started to get into the bible. When I read about the sufferings of the people in the bible, and how they received great joy, and I compare it with the joy of the Lord as I serve him, I begin to see the people that get mad at gospel preachers because they hate the message, are mad because they hate the Lord. I see it is that peace that passeth ALL understanding that brings the joy that is only increased in one's suffering for the Lord. My dear pastor friend, if you want strength, peace, stability, and intimacy with the Lord in your ministry you MUST endure the hardships. It is cleaving to the Lord that brings peace and joy.

21. For even hereunto were ye called: because Christ also suffered for us, leaving us an example, that ye should follow his steps: 22. Who did no sin, neither was guile found in his mouth: 23. Who, when he was reviled, reviled not again; when he suffered, he threatened not; but committed himself to him that judgeth righteously: 24. Who his own self bare our sins in his own body on the tree, that we, being dead to sins, should live unto righteousness: by whose stripes ye were healed. We are to use the example of the greatest sufferer of all. Jesus Christ endured all the way to glory. Jesus Christ had no sin in him, he did no wrong, he loved people yet they hated him. Jesus suffered and endured the cross and bore the pain and suffering of our sins so we, you and I, could have a way to heaven. He died for us so we could learn that relationship with God, so we can understand what it is like to love the Lord God with all our hearts, and that endurance is the strength behind our faith.

25. For ye were as sheep going astray; but are now returned unto the Shepherd and Bishop of your souls. The bible says here that we, Children of God were at one time going astray, we were lost, and that message of the gospel found us, it showed us the light, it drew us to Jesus. That message, the Holy

Bible, might not have gotten here if men and women before us did not endure their hardships. I say, might not, have gotten there because I believe God can use anyone he chooses to get this word out and man can never eliminate the gospel, but had those faithful men not endured, the spreading of the gospel might have been restricted.

1 Peter 1:7

That the trial of your faith, being much more precious than of gold that perisheth, though it be tried with fire, might be found unto praise and honour and glory at the appearing of Jesus Christ: The enduring of hardships, the trial of our faith is MORE precious than gold, Gold over time will perish but our faith will not. Our faith is strengthened through enduring. It is tested in the fire and found true. Enduring the hardships, trials, and testings, we are found unto the praise, and honor, and glory at the appearing of our Lord Jesus Christ.

Those that endure, not just in the pastorate, but in their walk with God, will be found blessed in the sight of God. These faithful saints will receive crowns that others will never be able to achieve. It is a blessing, not a curse, to suffer for the Lord, it is strength and integrity for the one that endures. Yes, the road is rough. Yes, the way is bumpy, but it is the Lord that blesses those that endure.

My dear reader friend, I know it seems like I slammed some pastors in this book, but that was not my intent. At the end of the day those that are not in the ministry for the Lord, but only for themselves, are only hurting the ministry, and driving people away from the Lord. Those pastors that are looking to quit, retire, or are focused on their exit plans, are only hindering the work of the Lord. It would be better for them to resign, and leave that pulpit empty so the Lord can fill it, then it would be for them to remain in their position and lead people to themselves. Think of it like in Revelation 3:16 where Jesus talks about being lukewarm, he spews lukewarm people out of his mouth, he wants nothing to do with people, especially pastors, that are lukewarm at best, all lukewarmness does is drive people away from the Lord

Again, the best fruit that any man-pleasing pastor can ever leave is, people seeking themselves, and not the Lord. The fruit that a God-called pastor leaves behind is people seeking God and not themselves. In order for this to happen, the pastor must hold the course, he must endure the hardships, and he must protect his church, and pulpit. They that endure to the end shall be saved. I will end this book with five words that I truly try to live by, when it comes to the bible.

IF I DO, HE WILL

You Are Loved

Pastor Chris Howe

Other books by the author:

Subject books:

The Office of Overseers: Biblical church leadership

Redemption: A True-Life Prodigal
(My personal Testimony)

The Genie god

The Biblical Family: from Beginning to Blended

The KJV is for Me: Why I use the King James Bible

Unguarded Gates: the Local Church

Reformed Theology: A Journey to Egypt

Commentaries: *Us Common Folks series*

Romans: For Us Common Folks

Acts: For Us Common Folks

I Corinthians: For Us Common Folks

II Corinthians: For Us Common Folks

Galatians: For Us Common Folks

To order any of my books please feel free to email me at sindestroys@gmail.com

All books are $10 each plus shipping, or $90 plus shipping for the entire set up to this book. (please identify which book you got this message from) as I add more books, the prices for the sets will change

www.ingramcontent.com/pod-product-compliance
Lightning Source LLC
LaVergne TN
LVHW050548160826
845677LV00011B/2230

9798847315128